The
Discerning
Parent

"How many books have you read on parenting? Whether your answer is none or too many, you should read this one. *The Discerning Parent* is a solid guide to parenting done the right way. After the first few chapters, I knew I was not simply going to endorse this book, I was going to pause, consider, and incorporate its insights into my own parenting. Tim and Sue Muldoon have done all parents a service with this gracefully written volume, a practical manual for raising holy young men and women."

Chris Stefanick
Founder of Real Life Catholic

"Tim and Sue Muldoon draw from the wisdom and spirituality of St. Ignatius of Loyola, whose reflections on discernment are a blessing to many in the Church today. As parents, they see how the practice of discernment sheds light on the task of parenting teens, who themselves are beginning the work of making important life decisions. I am grateful and so will you be for their insights on a discerning approach to family life."

Most. Rev. Robert P. Reed
Auxiliary Bishop of Boston
President of CatholicTV

"This is a book I wish I'd had for those challenging years of raising my own teen sons. Learn practical strategies and spiritual wisdom to help your favorite teens not only survive but thrive."

Lisa M. Hendey
Founder of *CatholicMom.com* and
author of *The Handbook for Catholic Moms*

"Tim and Sue Muldoon have done it again, welcoming readers on their family journey as they raise teenagers with faith, hope, love, and no little amount of courage. *The Discerning Parent* equips us with an Ignatian toolbox containing rich practices that include the daily examen and imaginative encounters with the scriptures. We are invited to explore our deepest desires for our children and attend to the ways in which God's 'slow work' is unfolding in their lives. Parents who are experiencing the many challenges that adolescence brings will find mercy and consolation here. Parents who are celebrating the joys that come with this stage of life will be encouraged to view these anew through the eyes of faith. The Muldoons are wise companions on this journey."

Mary M. Doyle Roche
Associate professor at College of the Holy Cross

The
Discerning
Parent

An Ignatian Guide to Raising Your Teen

Tim and Sue Muldoon

AVE MARIA PRESS AVE Notre Dame, Indiana

Founded in 1865, Ave Maria Press is a ministry of the United States Province of Holy Cross.

www.avemariapress.com

Paperback: ISBN-13 978-1-59471-689-8

E-book: ISBN-13 978-1-59471-690-4

Cover image © iStockphoto.

Cover design by Christopher D. Tobin.

Text design by Katherine Coleman.

Printed and bound in the United States of America.

Library of Congress Cataloging-in-Publication Data is available.

Contents

The Teen Years as a Discerning Age

The teen years are a discerning age, both for parents and teens* themselves. Both tweens and teens are in the process of weighing what they are learning from parents, peers, teachers, coaches, and the culture at large, making judgments about the kinds of persons they want to become. We parents must deal with how to support and challenge our growing children, how to recognize their increasing freedom, and how to stay part of their lives as they navigate difficult territory. Teens wrestle with some of the biggest questions that will stay with them their whole lives: whom and how to love, what to do with their lives, how to spend their time and money, what to do with their growing independence, what messages to accept or reject from popular culture, which public figures to emulate or critique, how to respond to sexual desires, and so many more. We parents must find a way to balance our hopes and our anxieties about our children.

---

*We'll use the word "teen" throughout the book. A teen is, strictly speaking, an adolescent between the ages of thirteen and nineteen. But we also have in mind tweens, who are somewhat younger (in age, maturity, or both) and who have one foot in childhood and the other in teenage-hood.

1

By describing teen years as *a discerning age*, we are calling to mind a rich theme in the tradition of Christian spirituality: careful listening to the voice of God, intimately present to those who develop what Jesus called "ears to hear" and "eyes to see." To discern is to consider carefully and to distinguish what is good from what is bad. The word comes from the Latin *dis-cernere*, meaning to separate or to sift. It suggests the image of a person who has a jar full of different-colored marbles and who must create neat groups of them according to color. It is slow work, involving careful observation, reflection, judgment, and action.

In Ignatian spirituality—that is, in the tradition of spiritual practices rooted in the writings of Saint Ignatius of Loyola—discernment is the practice of living reflectively, rooted in the desire to build our lives in cooperation with God. For those of us called to the vocation of parenting, that desire is twofold: it encompasses both the desire for ourselves to live faithfully and the desire for our children to become discerning adults.

Discernment might also be described as a process of developing the "acoustics of the heart," in the words of Wilkie Au and Noreen Cannon Au.[1] Discernment is a refinement of the practice of listening to God's music in a world full of noise. We love that image: it suggests that what each of us is doing in discernment is using a tuning fork to ensure that the tune we play is in harmony with the music of God. This book is an attempt to tune our own hearts as parents so that as we teach our teens, they too might live their lives in harmony with God.

The Discerning Parent includes our own reflections on the task of parenting, but it also reflects on surveys of teens and their parents that we conducted in preparation for the book. Our hope was to understand some of the shared challenges, triumphs, hopes, failures, obstacles, and helps that teens and their parents experience in the growing-up process. We'll share stories in the book using a character we'll call Kris, a composite of our own teens and those whom other parents have described to us. Our purpose is to share real stories without betraying confidentiality.

Our point is not to offer easy answers derived from the latest research. We've seen enough parenting guides over the years that vary widely in their recommendations—enough to know that easy answers may apply to some teens but not others. So the key to parenting teens, we are convinced, is not about knowing the latest research but about developing a discerning heart—and the latter can only be done through intentional practice (and God's grace!). To be sure, good research can help tune our hearts; much like technical know-how is part of tuning a piano; so we'll draw from some research to enhance our reflections. But the key, to carry the metaphor, is ultimately to develop a good ear for God's music by attending carefully to both God and our teens, to introduce them gradually and regularly to what living in harmony with God means. We'll put flesh on those bones in the chapters to come.

Throughout each chapter, we offer reflections based in both scripture and the human sciences, focusing on how to encourage our teens to develop a discerning approach to life. These reflections take seriously what we've learned from our experiences and from our surveys of others. The proverb "it is better to teach a man to fish than to give him a fish" hints at what we are after in these pages: modeling discernment and inviting teens to develop for themselves the skills of a discerning life, so that as they grow, their faith will grow with them. Too often we have encountered young adults whose faith development halted after the end of Confirmation classes and who have never developed an adult approach to faith. Our hope is that by sharing the practice of discernment described here, we all might be more confident in helping our teens to develop that practice in their own lives.

This is an opportunity to pause and consider our lives in the light of faith. Scripture is not a rule book; nor is it a book of magic spells. It is God's way of inviting us to hit the pause button on our busy lives and dwell within "God's time"—seeing things in the immediate foreground of life against the background of eternity. It is a chance to remind ourselves that all our struggles as parents, and all our hopes for our teens, unfold within a story of God creating us in love and calling us to grow in love to be more and more like him. That call is at once the most difficult and most meaningful way of living because it means we are willing to do the hard work of walking with our teens through the daily dramas of life. And with teens, there certainly are dramas! Turning to scripture reminds us, though, that these are but moments in a much larger story, and it is good to give ourselves regular reminders of that story.

We suggest taking some time with each chapter. If you are experienced at spiritual reading, this will be easy. If spiritual reading is new for you, or if it is something that you do only when you go to church, then consider these rules of thumb as a guide:

- There's no rush. When you read a book like this, it's different from reading an article online or a report from work. You're not trying to get to the end for "the point." Rather, there's an invitation to an experience.

It's a little bit like when a friend shows you a picture and tells an anecdote: you are interested in learning about the picture and reliving the experience with your friend. Seeing the picture might remind you of something in your own life or call to mind an interesting idea that you ponder for a bit. The same can be true of your experience here. It might be a good idea, then, to consider only one or two key insights from this book on a given day.

- Pay attention to how you feel. Remember that when you and a friend are talking, the important thing is that you're connecting. Your lives are enriched by each other's presence. Of course, not every conversation will be happy and easygoing. You'll talk about hard things, too: difficulties or successes at work or in your marriage, stories about your kids, plans for vacation, whatever. There is a richness in being honest with yourself in the presence of a friend, and that can happen only if you are paying attention to how you really feel about things.

- Let each chapter work on your imagination, and don't be afraid to go back to it again later. A meditation may point your consciousness in a direction that needs some time to unfold; don't be afraid to take it with you during the day, into conversation with a spouse or a friend, or into journaling.

- The total experience of reading, imagining, thinking, raising questions, and so on is the way that God speaks to us through scripture. The biblical text has a history and is, in itself, a precious gift to the Church. But when we call scripture "the Word of God," we mean it in a way analogous to the "word of a friend"—the important thing is the person who speaks the words. So use what follows to allow yourself to turn to God as the parent of a teen, looking for the consolation of a friend who seeks to support you in the important role of parenting.

In chapter 1, we begin by asking the broad question of how we can be good parents to our teens. We'll focus on the task of falling into God's rhythm—a metaphor for coming to live in a manner that is realistic about the way we have been created. We'll talk about the task of discernment as living within that rhythm and making good choices based on it. Finally, we'll address the way that discernment is a practice rooted in freedom, understood as living fully the life God has created us to live and through which we find our happiness.

In chapter 2, we'll explore Ignatian spirituality for wisdom about discernment, focusing on reflective practices that are relevant for parents of teens. What is particularly helpful about the Ignatian tradition is that it was and is an action-oriented spirituality, in contrast to earlier contemplative or monastic spiritualities. Ignatius was a layperson when he wrote his book *Spiritual Exercises*, and several of the people to whom he first gave the exercises were lay women and men. His guide to the spiritual life never assumed that a person had to enter a monastery or become a priest or member of a religious order. Instead, he saw the spiritual life as simply a reflective practice of a life lived in the ordinary, everyday world. The chapter will explore his vision of spirituality, and particularly discernment within that spirituality, with an eye to how parents of teens might benefit from it.

Chapter 3 is about helping teens become adept at building lives rooted in freedom. Our task is always and everywhere to help our teens understand our unflagging love for them, which provides the foundation that allows them to grow. Our love must be modeled on God's love: forgiving, merciful, and yet tough. This love allows us to see them in their full reality, unlike so many others who may see only what they want to see. It also means balancing the reality of who they are now with the reality of who they will become, helping them to develop a self-understanding that is not limited by the feedback they get from friends or the media. It concludes with a reflection on the importance of their regular participation in the liturgy of the Church, especially the Mass, if only to help them re-center their identity on their place within the Body of Christ.

Chapter 4 focuses on the ways teens act upon desires to become their best selves. Discernment can be described as the regular practice of sifting desires in order to understand which ones lead us to greatest freedom, and so this chapter will invite reflection on how we communicate what is most important in life, and what is ultimately worth desiring. It highlights the way we practice faith, in ways that make it visible to our teens that we seek to be guided by God.

Chapter 5 addresses one of the critical areas that parents worry about as their teens get older: how they regard and treat their bodies. Our reflections are rooted in a fundamental theology of Christ's incarnation, asking big questions about how that event shapes the way we think about what it means to be human, with flesh and blood. It goes on to explore some practical ways that teens raise their own questions about their bodies: sex, body art, exercise, body anxieties, and so on, and invites parents to consider how they might cultivate formative conversations about the importance of the body during a significant period of change in their teens' lives.

Chapter 6 is about parenting when life is hard. Most parents of teens we know can point to the struggles they have faced adjusting to life with their teens, and some can point to real heartaches. It is a reminder that our role as parents is not (and cannot be) ultimately about controlling our teens, but about being good stewards of the lives entrusted to us. It recalls Jesus' central ministry of healing, but it also calls to mind the way Jesus challenged his con-temporaries' injustices and even faced death for the sake of the Kingdom. In all things, the story of Jesus reminds parents that death and resurrection are written into the human story, and that faith in the God of Jesus Christ is a willingness to put even the worst of our experiences into the hands of One who has created us and loved us.

The conclusion offers an extended meditation that may help you gain perspective on what it means to parent teens with faith. You may want to return to this meditation, especially when life with your teen may be challenging.

At the end of the book, we point to some resources for further reading, surfing, and experiencing for the sake of your teen's formation. Now, please realize: by just reading this book, you are already making your prayers to God for your teen known. You are *doing* something. Our prayer for you is that this holy desire will be the seed of a fruitful relationship, even if those fruits come in different ways and on a different schedule from what you hope for. The stories of many saints point to the fact that our ways are not always God's ways and that the way God deals directly with his children—our teens—may be inaccessible to us. That is good news, for we must remind ourselves of the scope of what we can and cannot do. To paraphrase a line attributed to Saint Ignatius, we must pray as if our teens' well-being is up to us but act as if our teens' well-being is up to God.

Chapter One

How Can We Be Good Parents to Our Teens?

Ignatian Insight

An important practice in Ignatian spirituality is using our imagination in prayer, applying our five senses (seeing, hearing, tasting, touching, smelling) to a story from scripture in order to bring the story to life. This way of praying helps us treat the story not as information for our intellects to consider but as a living account told by a friend. It helps us to really feel the story and thereby to understand its meaning for our lives.

Consider the following story as a clue to the challenges of our teens' discerning age.

> The caravan rolled along across the dusty highway, heat rising up as the sun went down. The tired mother had spent much of the trip chatting with members of the extended family she rarely got to see; they were all enjoying the long trip home to the small town from

which they had set out days ago. The trip from the
capital took many hours, so they had decided to make
a virtue of necessity and spend the time catching up.

They had come to a rest stop, though, and so she
took some time to reconnect with her husband and
son, who were traveling just a few minutes ahead with
some neighbors. As she approached her husband, she
looked around, and asked where their son was. "What
do you mean?" he asked, surprised. "I thought he was
with you!"

"Jesus!" she screamed, more at the air than at him.
"We have to go back!"

This story is a slightly embellished telling of Luke's gospel
story about Jesus when he was a tween (twelve years old).
It's a story of miscommunication between an adolescent
and his parents. Yet it's also a story of how this miscommunication, this rushing back to locate a lost son, is about that
young son's new relationship with God the Father, and his
new role in the community of faith. Here is the way that
Luke, a Greek physician who learned about Jesus by following the apostle Paul, described the scene that followed:

> After three days they found him in the temple, sit-
> ting in the midst of the teachers, listening to them and
> asking them questions, and all who heard him were
> astounded at his understanding and his answers.
> When his parents saw him, they were astonished, and
> his mother said to him, "Son, why have you done this
> to us? Your father and I have been looking for you with
> great anxiety."
>
> And he said to them, "Why were you looking for
> me? Did you not know that I must be in my Father's
> house?" But they did not understand what he said to
> them. (Lk 2:46–50)

Prayer and Parenting

Can you feel Mary and Joseph's anxiety when you pray with this story? Have you ever had an experience with your teen that helps you to understand what they were feeling?

They did not understand what he said to them. How many times have you felt this when talking with your teen? Imagine the scene for a moment: You've just traveled for four days without having seen your son, and you're terrified that something terrible has happened to him. You're frantic, running around the city like you're mad, asking anyone and everyone where your son might be. Someone generously suggests "I think I might have seen him at the Temple, but I can't be sure," and you run there, hoping against hope that he's still okay.

Out of breath, you see him from a distance and nearly start crying with relief. Still shaken, you approach and yell to him. He acknowledges you, leaves the group of older men with whom he's been conversing, and says hello. Flabbergasted, your teary response is "Why have you done this to us? Your father and I have been looking for you!" He, though, is barely perturbed and wonders why you're making a big deal out of it.

Lest this telling of the story come across as too casual or (even worse) a little bit blasphemous, we point to a long tradition of imaginative prayer, which invites those reading scripture to imagine themselves as part of the story. Here we are inviting you to put yourself in the place of Mary or Joseph and see what happens when you imagine the scenes above.

Perspective Possibilities

Another way to imagine this story is to put yourself in the place of Jesus. What do you imagine was so compelling about staying in the Temple? What are you learning there? What makes you so focused on the conversation about God's Word that you forget about where your parents are?

Does seeing this story through the eyes of the teen Jesus suggest anything to you about your teen's perspective?

Pause and Consider

1. Can you identify with Mary and Joseph's frantic search, their perplexity, their concern?

2. Have you had experiences in which your growing child's behavior mystifies you, or even angers you?

3. What does it suggest to you to consider that Mary and Joseph, parents of God-in-human-flesh, felt these feelings?

Falling into God's Rhythm

This book is an invitation to discernment, the practice of carefully sifting through our feelings and our hopes, our fears and our plans, good cultural messages and not-so-good ones, all of which are involved in the ways that we live out our vocation as parents to teens. Think of it as a retreat in daily life, an attempt to hear God's music as you wrestle with how to be a good parent to your teen. Our focus will be on developing a keen spirituality, well attuned to the way that God is present in our decision-making.

We come to the question of discernment very self-ishly: we too are trying to practice it in the midst of raising three teens: two girls and a boy. We have spent much effort in our professional lives—Sue as a counselor and religious educator, Tim as a theologian, professor, and spiritual director—working with teens and their parents in high school and college. But it is a different matter to take the best professional conversations and distill them in ways appropriate for our own children. To use an analogy, good doctors may know everything about cutting-edge prevention and treatment, but that doesn't mean they can keep members of their own families from getting the flu or breaking a leg. So this book is our effort to think through and pray about what we've learned in order to share some ideas about how to parent our teens with faith. In preparation for this book, we took informal surveys of parents and teens who shared with us what they have learned about faith over the years. We'll share what we've learned, both from parents and teens as well as from our professional work.

In our previous book, *Six Sacred Rules for Families*, we described parenting and family life as a shared pilgrimage: a sacred journey that families walk together, toward God. That same image is helpful here, and much of what we wrote there applies to parenting teens. But a key difference is that teens, as they grow older, become aware of different directions they want their pilgrimages to take. Notice that Luke's story of Jesus as a tween was an example of that: he was developing a new sense of self, and his choice to remain in the Temple, while rooted in a good intention, left his parents wondering where he was. Parents understand teens' need to distance themselves from their parents and to develop unique personalities, and so the work of sharing the pilgrimage becomes more and more difficult. The task of parenting becomes a task of careful, shared discernment. Practicing what we preach means constantly remembering that a life of sharing faith with teens means reciprocity: challenging the ways our teens live, as well as allowing our teens to challenge the ways we live. Saint Benedict's famous Rule includes the reminder that "it is often to the younger that the Lord reveals what is better."

How are we to navigate this new period of our children's lives? When our oldest daughter began high school, we were both struck at how sudden was the change in our relationship with her, simply because of how much time she spent away from home. On the one hand, we were happy that she found engaging things to be involved in at school. She had a lot of work to do, and practices and games kept her there late. But on the other hand, it began to feel almost as though she had already left for college. We missed her. And with two other children vying for our attention, it would have been pretty easy to leave her to her own devices (figuratively speaking, but also literally, since she is never without her phone). At a certain point, prompted in part by some concerns that she was becoming withdrawn from our family dynamics, we picked her up after school and—in spite of her protests—took her out for pizza. The result was like unclogging a drain: we had a long conversation about many things, and we all left feeling renewed and hopeful. Simply making time to be alone with our daughter sent the very clear signal that we wanted to be present to her even as she was growing more independent.

Teaching discernment means practicing discernment. This book is an invitation to becoming more discerning people so that we can model for our teens what it means to be discerning. On a very basic level, that means becoming practiced in the art of mindfulness: awareness of who we are and what kinds of people we choose to become, especially amid a world of bombarding information. On a deeper level, that means becoming practiced in the art of prayer—the daily conversation with a God whose invitation to the fullness of life is offered through a deepening friendship with Jesus. In Catholic tradition, discernment is rooted in daily practices of faith. Allow us to share one illustration.

Leah Libresco is a twentysomething Catholic writer, and one interesting part of her story is that before she entered the Church, she blogged prominently as an atheist. Her very public conversion story led her to write a book about her experience called *Arriving at Amen*, in which she recounts her wonder at discovering what prayer was all about. Having been raised without any religion, everything about prayer was new to her, and she wrote of her particular difficulty grasping a traditional prayer like the Rosary. In an interview with *America* magazine, she described the process this way.

> When I started learning to waltz, I spent a lot of time just practicing the basic waltz step—the same kind of endless repetition as the Hail Marys of the Rosary. The reason I was supposed to keep practicing was so that my feet could keep the rhythm, no matter what.
>
> Since I'm a follow when I dance, I don't need to have learned every step to be able to dance it—usually, if I have a good enough connection with my partner and a reasonable grasp of the basic, I can follow my

lead through more complicated steps than I could execute alone, since their motion leads me into the next place I should be.

I wound up thinking of the rosary as my chance to follow a "basic step" for prayer. My goal wasn't to produce epiphanies about the lives of Christ and Mary, but to fall into God's rhythm and to be ready to move if he led me.[1]

That's a great image: "falling into God's rhythm." It recalls the earlier "acoustics of the heart" that we pointed to. Both of these images suggest a good way to approach prayer, both in our own lives and in what we hope to convey to our teens: namely, that it is about playing along with a God who is near if we but ask him to be.

The key to discernment, then, is the desire to do it. Ours is a world of a lot of noise, and so it is easy for us— and even easier for our teens—to become distracted. God's voice is often the "light silent sound" rather than the wind, earthquake, or fire.

> There was a strong and violent wind rending the mountains and crushing rocks before the LORD—but the LORD was not in the wind; after the wind, an earthquake—but the LORD was not in the earthquake; after the earthquake, fire—but the LORD was not in the fire; after the fire, a light silent sound. When he heard this, Elijah hid his face in his cloak and went out and stood at the entrance of the cave. (1 Kgs 19:11–13)

Your Spiritual Self

Can you identify with Elijah in this story? Have you experienced God as a "light silent sound" in the midst of a busy life?

Let's face it: in a world where wind, earthquakes, and fire draw crowds, sell tickets, drive market share, invite page views, garner "likes," and have sex appeal, the light silent sound of God often pales in comparison. (Cue the slow motion eye-rolls as you imagine this advice to your teen: "Hey, get off your screen for a few minutes and let's listen to God together!") So we will try to be practical. While there are some young people whom God seems to touch in unique ways, drawing them into lives of deep prayer and service, many are more likely to follow the crowd. And much of the crowd, at least in the teens and twenties, tends to move away from organized religion. So we have two tasks as parents:

1. Interrupt the natural tendencies of teens to go along with the crowd.

2. Provide opportunities where there might be a fruitful place in their hearts for God.

The first task applies to all parents aiding in the normal personality development of adolescents. The second is the one that we'll develop in greater detail in the course of this book.

One recent story from our own experience as parents sheds light on these two tasks. A couple of years ago, we started participating in a parish effort called the Boston Sock Exchange, which was founded by a priest some years ago. Several local parishes agree to take one Saturday each month to head down to the Boston Common to distribute food, clothing, and other items to homeless men and women. We wanted to establish a practice of direct engagement with people in situations of need and so told Kris that he and his mom would be going. Not surprisingly, he refused. He had plans to meet friends that day. He objected that there would be no one else his age there. It would be boring. We insisted, though, and after much wrangling—including an 8:00 wake-up call on a Saturday—we managed to get him out the door.

The three-hour commitment included a good deal of busy work, moving items to cars, driving downtown, and setting up, followed by an hour and a half of engaging directly with the population everyone was there to serve. Happily, there were other teens there to help, so Kris did not feel quite so alone in the effort. The time passed quickly, and everyone headed home. To his great credit, while on the way home he remarked, "I actually kind of liked that." He had been nudged out of his comfort zone and discovered something new there.

We've taken a couple of important lessons from that experience. The first is that there is no substitute for actual, concrete experience. No amount of talking about the poor could have substituted for real experience with real human beings who experience poverty. We won't bore you with theories of developmental psychology about why this is the case; suffice it to say that at their stage of becoming adults, lived experience is critical. To put it slightly differently, what we are doing with our teens can be summed up in a pithy truism that applies as much to parenting as it does to public speaking or writing, or any other attempt at persuasion: *Show, don't tell.* Show your teen what your faith is; don't just talk about it. If you have faith that serving others is important, give them experiences in which you share service. If you have faith that generosity is better than selfishness, give them experiences in which to be generous with their time, effort, or money. If you have faith that God is good and that worship is the appropriate response, go to church with them. And so on. What are the bedrock truths by which you have come to build your life? How can you give your teen experiences that help them to own those bedrock truths?

Take Away

Consider writing down what you consider bedrock truths. What are the most important lessons you want your teen to learn? And what are the concrete experiences that will help them learn those lessons?

The second lesson is that sharing faith with a teen will almost certainly involve pushback. From their perspective, to quote a bumper sticker, "If it's not fun, why do it?" Our consumerist culture wants to persuade adults to be more like teens rather than vice versa, because those motivated by fun are easier to sell things to. The cultural message is that adulthood is boring; you should put yourself first; entertainment is fun; and so on. As teens naturally distance themselves from their parents for the sake of self-understanding, they will gravitate toward the things their friends embrace, especially entertainment. In such a context, to them, any substantial lessons about life are likely to appear dreary and pointless. Aristotle observed over two millennia ago that the young are likely to find happiness in pleasure, in part because they have not yet had the training in habits of life that afford more lasting happiness. Pleasure is to happiness what simple sugars are to a diet: they offer a temporary high, followed by a crash, unless they are accompanied by something more complex.

Sharing your faith with your teen is similar to what you taught them about eating when they were toddlers. Then, you expected pushback when you insisted that vegetables are better than candy. Now, you must expect pushback when you suggest that it is important to practice generosity or to pray. Be persistent.

We must practice what we preach. We must be willing to be part of our teens' lives, walking with them, in order to share our faith, our way of living. Our great hope is that by sharing a pilgrimage with our teens, we will help them to discern a living God who is walking with them, whose Holy Spirit guides them to make choices rooted in generous love. We hope that they will come to know Jesus as the one who came to show the way to the Father, by demonstrating the way of love. We hope that they will come to see the Church as the body of believers dedicated to living out the example of Jesus and being the ongoing presence of Jesus in the world, sanctifying the world in a manner analogous to the presence of yeast in bread. We hope to enliven their imaginations in ways that excite them to discern who God has made them to be, with a growing mindfulness of their giftedness. Finally, we hope that they will share these same gifts with the Church, drawing hope from the people gathered there, all of whom are blessed and broken in the sharing of the Eucharist to be a gift to the world.

For Reflection and Conversation

1. Have you been surprised by your teen's desire for inde-
    pendence? What are some ways you might creatively
    reconnect with your teen?

2. Can you talk with your teen about God? If this is not easy, can you talk about what he or she hopes for in life or about what is most meaningful?

3. What elements of your teen's world might you use to start a conversation—music, TV, movies, sports, or something else? How might you show interest in entering your teen's world and learning his/her perspective on it?

Our Teens' Happiness

What we are sharing in these pages are the ways that we are trying to be faithful to God's call to us to be parents. We are very much in the midst of that vocation; we cannot claim the wisdom of hindsight. We rely on others who have written and researched about family life, as well as others who are masters of the spiritual life or have insights about living as faithful followers of Jesus. What is important in learning discernment, and what we have come to understand in our own lives, is that it is impossible to have absolute certainty about the way that our decisions—or decisions made for our children—will turn out. Practicing discernment does not guarantee happiness, nor does it guarantee that our children will get into the best universities or make lots of money. Nor does it guarantee that our children will always choose to practice their faith. Practicing discernment means meditating on the presence of God in our lives, sustaining us both in our times of joy and in our times of challenge or sorrow. To paraphrase the spiritual writer William Barry, S.J., discernment is not a guarantee of avoiding anything that we fear, but knowing that even if what we fear happens, God is with us in the midst of it.

Similarly, in practicing discernment with our teens, we cannot guarantee that they will always choose what we would choose. We know many good parents who diligently sought to guide their children through religious education only to find that as adults they do not practice their faith. In the various times we have spoken to groups of parents (and grandparents), we have listened to how painful that can be. Yet we are quick to remind them that faith is more complex than religious practice. We'll expand on this point later, pointing to questions like how much to require your teens to go to Mass or Confession. But underneath those more specific questions is a more foundational point: discernment is ultimately about a dynamic relationship with God that unfolds over the course of a lifetime, always predicated on the freedom of the person and the freedom of God. What that means practically is that while parents can help shape the ways that teens respond to God's invitation into friendship, ultimately it is up to God to "deal directly with the creature," in the words of Saint Ignatius. God is free to act in our teens' lives, and our teens are ultimately free to say yes or no to the various ways God is working to invite them. Our role is to be faithful to our vocation as parents: to pray for our children, to educate them, to lead them toward good choices. Perhaps the way they are responding to God is still hidden to us and will reach fruition after we have died. Part of our faith, our discernment, means allowing that relationship to unfold.

Pause and Consider

1. How do you see God dealing directly with your teen? What are the ways you see emerging signs of

generosity, thinking of others, hopefulness, creativity, giftedness?

2. Do you see examples of your teen coming up with new ideas about how to spend time and energy? Does your teen make plans for vacations or weekends? Does your teen feel the freedom to make such plans?

Why We Go the Extra Mile

One temptation we have discovered in parenting is that as teens get older, it becomes easier to think of them as adults. They want more freedom and have greater ability to find it: whether by spending much of their time with friends or spending time at home alone in a room (perhaps attached to some form of technology, communicating with friends). With their growing autonomy, they will have greater management of their time and, eventually, their money. Yet we and the parents we surveyed agree that it is imperative to still *parent* teens, perhaps now more than ever. "Keep them close," wrote one parent. Keep an eye on who their friends are and who their friends' parents are. Monitor whether there is adult supervision when they are invited to a friend's home. And stay involved with them; do not let their growing autonomy dissuade you from being present in their lives.

We will introduce here a distinction that we'll address in greater detail later: the difference between autonomy and freedom. *Autonomy*, which means "self rule" in Greek, is a word that describes the growing desire of teens to live their own lives and not be under the constant control of parents, as perhaps they might see that their younger siblings are. Autonomy is the natural result of growing older and gaining a sense of oneself in the world. It comes from increased abilities to understand the world they live in, and a growing sense of their power. We want to cultivate autonomy in our children; a good deal of research supports the idea that kids and teens need to develop enough self-understanding so as not to be reliant on their parents as they get older.[2]

But autonomy is not freedom. The growing ability to make choices for oneself is far from a guarantee that those choices will be good and will lead to a happy life. To use one example: as teens progress through driver's education, they gain a good deal more hope for autonomy as they imagine what they will be able to do when they drive. But as adults, we know that they need close supervision. We demand that they study and take a test to understand the rules of the road before they are allowed to get behind the wheel. And when they start driving, it is with an adult and without peer pressure. Eventually they gain experience, developing habits that we hope will become cemented in their consciousness—and only after a period of practice do we allow them to drive on their own or with friends.

What this example illustrates is a relationship between autonomy and freedom, understood as the power to secure for oneself those goods that will bring about lasting happiness. Note the paradox: we limit teens' autonomy as they develop, so that they will be able eventually to discover freedom. This same pattern applies to other kinds of ways we hope to form our teens: we curb their autonomy in various areas so that they learn patterns of living that lead to freedom. Examples include placing limits on things—such as technology use, time apart from family, or purchases—as well as mandating practices like going to Mass, doing homework, and serving others. Teens need to be parented well because the stakes are higher as they develop autonomy: mistakes can be serious and even life altering. Not only in driving, but also making choices around sex, alcohol or drug use, or school can affect them for the rest of their lives, positively or negatively.

What we hope for our teens is a growing freedom: that is, we hope that they will use their autonomy in ways that promote their well-being and the well-being of others. Freedom, rightly understood, is fully embracing who God has created us to be. We want our teens to develop the critical skills that will help them to discern the meaning of strong cultural messages—many of which are harmful—in order that they might discover the reality of who they are and embrace their lives as gifts to be celebrated and shared with others. We can play an important part in helping them develop a positive autonomy that helps them respond to God's invitation to freedom. We can help them pay attention to what the early Christian philosopher Justin Martyr described as "seeds of the Word" in culture: hints of Christ and the fullness of truth one can learn to see in the world. Helping our teens to discern these seeds of the Word will help them to develop a critical eye toward what they see others around them doing.

For Reflection and Conversation

1. What have been some times in your teen's life when you have sensed him/her being most happy?

2. What sort of freedom do you imagine for your teen? What do you hope your teen will be good at—and be willing to work for?

Chapter Two

Learning from Ignatius

As we noted earlier, Ignatian spirituality is a practical approach to prayer, with an eye to how a close friendship with God might impact the way we live our lives and relate to others. What motivated Saint Ignatius was a call to help ordinary people to live life to the fullest by drawing closer to God and understanding who God created them to be.

To us, that motivation strikes home. We have desires for that kind of authenticity and meaning, and we certainly hope for it for our kids. Minimally, we hope that our lives will be built on something more lasting than public opinion or political expediency—and we hope our kids will similarly develop a strong desire for authentic lives. We hope to become discerning, to develop the habit of finding the good, the true, and the beautiful in our experiences and acting upon great and holy desires that reflect the work that God wants to do in the world through our lives.

In this chapter, we'll explore what we've learned about parenting from Ignatian spirituality. We'll pay attention to Saint Ignatius himself, since his own life tells the story of how he came to understand discernment, but will then go on to share how what we've learned from his example is helpful to us as parents.

Ignatian Insight

Ignatian spirituality is rooted in imagining what it would be like to be asked directly by Jesus to be part of building God's kingdom in the concrete circumstances of your life. Saint Ignatius himself experienced what it meant to take on such a strong sense of mission in life, and we can learn much from his example.

Iñigo, as he was first called, came from Loyola, a place in the Basque region of northern Spain. He grew up around the turn of the sixteenth century, a time that, in historical retrospect, was the hinge between the medieval and modern worlds. When he wrote his autobiography late in life, against his own wishes but at the urging of younger followers, he observed that his own adolescence lasted until he was twenty-six. Up to that point, he wrote, he was "enthralled by the vanities of the world"—military exploits, prestige and honor, charm with women. His imagination was shaped by the chivalric romances of figures like Montalvo's Amadís of Gaul, a figure whom readers of English might compare to those found in the stories of King Arthur.

Ignatius points to the important influence of imagination in his spiritual life. Like teens today, young Iñigo latched onto what was popular, drawing ideas about himself from the heroes that were lionized among his contemporaries. His autobiography begins with the story of how that imagination held sway over his identity. He became what he imagined—a soldier—and was able to live within that fantasy until a life-changing event made it literally blow up in his face.

That event was a battle, where he urged his commander to continue a hopeless fight. We can envision the kind of chest-thumping bravado that one still sees today on a football field or in a war-themed movie—Iñigo imagined himself as the warrior ready to die for glory. But the result was neither death nor glory; it was a disfiguring wound to his leg, one that left him bedridden and broken for months.

Adolescent fantasies die hard. For Iñigo, the wound was both physically and emotionally excruciating. When doctors discovered that the wound had set badly, they broke the leg again and reset it. But Iñigo was upset by the fact that the result was a grotesque lump under the knee and one leg shorter than the other—intolerable for one who expected to live a courtly life among nobles. He asked doctors to open the wound again, cut the bone, and then stretch the leg. He could not let go of the desire for the life he still clung to in his imagination.

Ignatius's later reflections on what today is called a "quarter-life crisis" shed light on how he came to understand discernment—and how we might consider through a discerning lens the challenges facing our teens. For young Iñigo, the period of convalescence was rooted in the basic question: *What kind of a person am I?* At that time, Iñigo did not have the spiritual and theological vocabulary to help him name what was going on; he could speak only of the ways that he felt when he imagined different possibilities. Iñigo could express his complex inner life in only rudimentary affective terms: he was happy or sad, at peace or feeling distracted. Early on, he asked for what nearly every adolescent would ask for when laid up in bed for months at a time: distraction. For him, that meant reading the usual chivalric stories that populated the imaginative world in which he chose to make his home. They provided excitement and adventure, emotional responses that could take his mind away from the grim reality of his shattered life.

But there were no such stories at hand where he convalesced. If a contemporary version of Iñigo's story were written today, it would involve someone recuperating in a place with no computers, screens, or phones—only an old library of religious books. For the only books that Iñigo could lay his hands on were those about the saints and the life of Christ. And while he does not include these details in his autobiography, we imagine him complaining for days about the meager resources.

Iñigo found himself forced into what today we might describe as a retreat—a withdrawal from everyday concerns and the usual sources of daily conversation and a chance to let one's imagination run freely. Lacking any discernible piety at the time, but bored stiff, Iñigo turned to the books at hand just to pass the time. What he found was that they began to work on his imagination in ways that he did not expect.

Let us quote him directly, highlighting the fact that he remembered the details decades later. These experiences helped Iñigo begin to understand discernment—so much so that the mature Ignatius wanted to share his story in order that his younger followers might begin to practice discernment by reflecting on their own experiences in similar ways. Note that in this selection from his autobiography, he uses the third person, later calling himself "the pilgrim" as he dictated his memories to a secretary.

> As he read them over many times, he became rather fond of what he found written there. But interrupting his reading, he sometimes stopped to think about the things he had read and at other times about the things of the world that he used to think of before. . . . He imagined what he would do in the service of a certain lady; the means he would take so he could go to the place where she lived; the quips—the words he would address to her; the feats of arms he would perform in her service. . . .
>
> Nevertheless Our Lord assisted him, by causing these thoughts to be followed by others that arose from the things he read. For in reading the life of Our Lord and of the saints, he stopped to think, reasoning within himself, "What if I should do what St. Francis did, and what St. Dominic did?" . . . These thoughts also lasted a good while; then, other things coming in between, the worldly ones mentioned above returned, and he also stayed long with them. . . .
>
> Yet there was this difference. When he was thinking of those things of the world he took much delight in them, but afterwards, when he was tired and put them aside, he found himself dry and dissatisfied. But when he thought of going to Jerusalem barefoot, and of eating nothing but plain vegetables and of practicing all the other rigors that he saw in the saints, not only was he consoled when he had these thoughts, but even after putting them aside he remained satisfied and joyful.[1]

Iñigo learned discernment by beginning to pay attention to the contrast between what he liked to imagine—that late medieval fantasy of chivalric life as knight—and what the stories of holy lives elicited in his imagination. The seed of his discernment was the insight: "I feel better when I imagine being like the saints than when I imagine being a knight." Note, though, that his opportunity for discernment did not happen autonomously. He did not plan to have an opportunity to weigh the differences between a chivalric life and a religious life; that opportunity arose when he was forced to slow down and reflect. Paradoxically, it was relinquishing autonomy, that ability to make choices about his life, that allowed him to discover a new path to freedom.

Ask Yourself

1. What are some of the different ways you imagined yourself when you were a teen and young adult?

2. Who are the key people today, alive or dead, who influence your understanding of the person you want to be?

Discovering Freedom

Following his discernment that God was calling him to live in imitation of Christ and the saints, Iñigo entered a turbulent period. On the one hand, he found himself desiring to do what the great saints had done; on the other, he was remorseful over his sins and desired to undertake severe penance. Later, when he went off to a cave outside the town of Manresa to compose his Spiritual Exercises, he articulated these difficulties. In a section in which he describes rules for discernment, he observes first that "the enemy of our nature"—the devil—proposes apparent pleasures, much like he had experienced in his life as a soldier. The pleasures are temporary, rooted in facsimiles of authentic desire—they give some good feelings but then wither away because they have no depth. Second, he observes that once a person resolves to do good, cleansing himself or herself of sin and "rising from good to better in the service of God our Lord," the evil spirit puts up all sorts of obstacles and false reasons why the person couldn't possibly go on. It seems Iñigo experienced these obstacles frequently, waiting for the Lord's consolation to quiet his soul and offer comfort and reassurance that his path was the right one.

For Ignatius, discernment unfolded in the context of a battle between God and the enemy for his soul. Discernment, then, is the process by which we come to know the interior movements of our souls and come to recognize when we are drawn by a desire rooted in God or a desire rooted in the work of the enemy. To use a biblical image, the human soul is a field in which both the weeds and the wheat take root, growing together until harvest time. The discerning heart is one that can carefully separate weeds from wheat in order to bring forth the greatest amount of fruit. It is a practice by which we come to reap the fruit of prayer and live more fully as the persons God has created us to be, unswayed by the false desires proposed by the enemy.

What is central in Ignatius's understanding of the human heart is that it is a creation of a loving God, who draws a person into free, unmediated relationship. In his advice to those who give the Exercises to others, he says that it is vital that the spiritual director not get in God's way; God must deal directly with the creature and vice-versa. That advice is equally true for parents; no one can take God's place. What, then, is a parent's task, particularly when seeing a son or daughter falling prey to the "apparent pleasures" that Ignatius writes about? His answer is that in the midst of a person moving from one pleasure to the other, the good spirit stings the conscience through reason. The task of a parent is analogous: the parent seeks always to articulate what is reasonable and good, at times being willing to sting a teen's conscience. But ultimately, it is the parent's task to open the way toward freedom, even though the teen must ultimately choose it for himself or herself. That process may be easy, but it may also be hard and stretch out for years. But the task of discernment ultimately falls on each of us —individually loved and created by God.

Ask Yourself

1. Have you ever made choices based on what appeared to bring pleasure but over time turned out to meet dead-ends? What made you "come to your senses"?

2. Can you identify with Ignatius's idea that there is a kind of tug-of-war between the good and the bad in the human heart? In what ways have you experienced this kind of inner struggle?

Some Ignatian Tools for Discernment

After his conversion, Ignatius felt his way forward as a follower of Jesus, often unsure of what God was calling him to do. He describes many of his missteps in the autobiography, as if to suggest to younger disciples that the decision to be a Christian does not automatically bring with it clarity about a life direction. He thought he might want to be a monk, or a beggar, or a pilgrim en route to Jerusalem. He found himself experiencing inner turmoil but did not yet understand the discernment process. Eventually, his decision to go to Manresa was motivated by a desire to spend time alone with God, and it was during that experience that he wrote his Spiritual Exercises.

Ignatius's book is a collection of various types of meditative and imaginative prayers, organized into four weeks. He wrote them as a guide for those who might lead people through a way of developing greater intimacy with God, offering various comments on how the Exercises might be adapted to people in different life circumstances. For someone serious about discerning a call to marriage or religious life, for example, Ignatius offers a thirty-day silent retreat. For those engaged in life as a student, a parent, or a busy professional, he offers different exercises, which might stretch out over a much longer period of time in ordinary life.[2]

The attraction to Ignatian spirituality—which we've seen grow over the years, with many books, websites, apps, programs, and retreats dedicated to applying it to people from every walk of life—has a great deal to do with this adaptability that Ignatius envisioned. His earliest retreatants were his own college roommates, and after he and his friends were ordained to the priesthood, he offered the Exercises to a number of laypeople, including several women. His great desire, as he wrote, was to "help souls"—that is, to give people the opportunity to prayerfully encounter a God who was to be found in all things.

There is a worldliness to Ignatius's spirituality: unlike other traditions, which emphasize removal from the world, his spirituality amounts to a kind of immersion in the world and an attentiveness to where God is alive in it. For parents, the immediate value of this tradition is that it is fundamentally about helping our teens to discover what the Jesuit poet Gerard Manley Hopkins called "the dearest freshness deep down things"—the reality underneath appearance. Perhaps that means taking a fifteen-second period of silence before we share grace before meals or ending the day by remembering the people we've encountered who need our prayers. It might mean seeking out opportunities to serve the poor (whether or not service hours are required for school!) or reaching out to a neighbor or friend who is going through a difficult time. We hope that simply calling to mind who God wants us to be for others offers our teens an example of how to live that is different from those which appear to us to be more self-focused or harmful.

One specific Ignatian practice is the examen, a practice of prayerfully reflecting on the past day. It's one that we practice in different ways and encourage others to practice. One example is to go over the past twenty-four hours, focusing on all the things for which we want to give God thanks, from the most obvious (such as a kindness shown to us) to the more hidden (such as having clean water to drink). Another example is to simply walk through the past twenty-four hours in our imaginations, paying attention to the various emotions that our experiences have elicited. We've found that sometimes doing that with our teens can elicit from them remembrance of someone they want to pray for.[3]

Your Spiritual Self

When you do an examen, don't just remember the past day. First, thank God for being present in your life. Second, pray for light, asking to see your day through God's eyes. Next, walk through the past twenty-four hours. Then pick one particular experience and talk with Jesus directly about what it means. Bring your emotions into the conversation, and allow yourself to ask forgiveness or to express joy. Close with a short prayer, resolving to bring your insights into the next twenty-four hours.

Another important practice has to do with the importance of imagination. Ignatius invites retreatants into specific imaginative exercises, such as an imagination of how God in heaven sees the entirety of creation. What Ignatius was interested in was eliciting not only a cool, disinterested observation of the world, but a passionate, felt understanding of things. For parents, maybe that means a readiness to start conversation with teens about dramas unfolding at school or work, or difficult social problems in the world, or things that move us toward happiness or anger. We want our teens to "befriend their desires."[4] We want them to understand what it means to feel warmed by the friendly words of a stranger, saddened at the stories of crime or terrorism, outraged at expressions of racism or xenophobia, consoled by acts of kindness, emboldened to act by a deep sense of their giftedness, and so on. Using Jesus' parables to talk about current events, or talking about the weekly readings on the way to Mass, is our way of populating our teens' imaginations with images from scripture.

We'll mention one final word about what we learn from Ignatius as parents of teens: faith is ultimately rooted in practices rather than ideas. Ignatius observed that love is shown more in deeds than in words, and we are suggesting a similar point. Our faith is ultimately manifest in our willingness to love the way Jesus did: to go out of our way to find the lost, the broken, and the marginalized, and to

extend healing. We hope that our teens see faith in action—
in the ways that we treat them and others—and are drawn
to it. The human heart is created for love and thrives when
it acts in the image of God's own heart. "Heart speaks to
heart," wrote Saint Francis de Sales, describing the intimacy of the soul with God. The heart is drawn to God
naturally, and so our role is to open experiences that allow
for this natural attraction to take place. For a few young
people, that may happen in Mass or other explicitly religious practices. More often, it happens elsewhere, when
they become alive to the ways their hearts are moved. We
can help them to reflect, understand, and act upon their
nascent desires to do what is good and even—if they come
to name it—serve God with their whole hearts. The first
way that we can provide the foundation for that dynamic
to unfold in their lives is to love them the way God loves
us.

Ask Yourself

1. What practices nourished your faith as you grew up?

2. What do you do today to nourish your relationship
   with God? What practices nourish your faith, whether
   they are explicitly religious or not?

Chapter Three

Helping Them Build Their Lives

I praise you, because I am wonderfully made;
wonderful are your works! My very self you
know.

PSALM 139:14

One of the most important developmental tasks that all
teens must face is the construction of a strong sense of
self that is lovable and capable of loving others. Modern
psychology and the Bible have shown us that lack of this
strong sense of self can lead to violence, directed either
toward the self or toward others. Think of the stories of
Cain and Abel, Joseph and the brothers who sell him into
slavery, or Jacob and Esau—all these are stories of siblings
who vie for a parent's attention and who, lacking a strong
sense of being completely loved and cherished for who
they are, make choices that lead them to harm to themselves or their loved ones. Today, bullying (and cyberbully-
ing), aggressive competition, use of drugs and alcohol, and

manipulative expressions of sexuality are some examples of behaviors that can arise from an unformed sense of self.

Ignatian Insight

One fruit of praying the Ignatian examen is learning to see our teens the way God does, wholly loved and cherished, gifted to do some good in the world.

The first job of a parent at every stage of a child's life, from infancy through adulthood, is to manifest an unshakable love for their children. Every parent knows what a difficult balancing act this can be, especially as kids grow into their teens. Finding the right mix of comfort and challenge can be difficult. How can we steer them toward decisions that will benefit them and others while at the same time make them aware of the consequences of bad decisions? How can we help them develop a disciplined approach to life—from school to friend choices, from drugs and alcohol to sex, from work to use of time? How can we discipline lovingly while always letting them know that we love them unconditionally? In this chapter, we look at several stories from the scriptures that suggest ways of meditating and praying about finding this balance.

Establishing Roots

The gospels begin with a long description by Matthew of forty-two generations from Abraham to Jesus. We might rush through these names, but experts are quick to point out that they tell a story of how Jesus comes from a line that begins with Abraham, includes the great king David, and culminates in the Messiah. In other words, Matthew is making a point: Jesus has a history that is the very history of God's careful involvement with the people of Israel. This genealogy shapes the story that Matthew wants to tell about Jesus: the story of a man whom God has promised to his chosen people and whose life is a fulfillment of the hopes of generations. Much of Matthew's gospel is dedicated to showing the way that Jesus fulfills these hopes, and he regularly points back to the writings of the prophets to illustrate them.

The message Matthew offers is clear: even God has a family tree. Even God, author of the universe, enters human history with a past that shapes who he becomes. Even God has a life that is not entirely his own; it is a gift that emerges when a teen girl says yes to the angel, after generations and generations of ancestors have lived out the lives that God gave them.

This strong emphasis on genealogy suggests a point for parents to consider. Awareness of one's family tree does not come naturally to teens. Because of many social factors today, they are subject to a developmental stage characterized by egocentrism: that is, they see themselves as the center of the world, unconnected to a longer story of where they have come from. Perhaps you've already witnessed this: obsession with appearance, even for minor excursions outside the home; panic at being seen with parents in public; terror of minor mishaps like tripping, fearing that the world is always watching them; and so on. From an adult perspective, these behaviors may seem extreme, but they are characteristic of normal adolescent development. They are part of the task of growing up.

Adults can help teens accomplish that task by calling to mind that they are part of a longer story of the work that

God is doing in the world. Gentle reminders—not in times of stress, but rather as part of everyday conversation—that they are embedded within a larger community, with history, can help them come to terms with an emerging adult sense of their place in the world.

As parents of adopted children, we know that conversations about genealogy, particularly at school, can be difficult. Adoptive parents of younger children, especially, often dread "family tree" or "when I was born" assignments, which highlight the difference they feel from other kids in class. On the other hand, considering one's family tree as a teen can be a reminder that their lives are part of a longer story in which God has been active—a story in which, it is important to recall, Jesus himself had an adoptive father. The key point is not about blood relations, as important as those can be, but about having a sense of belonging within a family.

Benoît Talleu, a French eighteen-year-old who was adopted from Vietnam as an infant, expresses this importance of genealogy beautifully. His sensibility about being adopted into a different culture makes a point applicable to all children.

> An orphan child without parents is a child deprived from its roots, and it is very important to give some new roots in a new family that becomes theirs. It is a very peculiar thing, because we just transplant someone to a genealogical tree that is not theirs to start with, but that eventually becomes it. I became a son with a name, a story, with ancestors, with parents, with brothers and sisters.[1]

Benoît highlights a point that he, as an adoptee, has come to understand in ways that many teens do not—namely, that one of the deep graces of family life is belonging within a longer family story, a genealogy. It is interesting to note, by the way, that even Jesus' own family tree is not without strange branches. Matthew makes a point of including in his genealogy some of Jesus' ancestors who were disreputable or from despised foreign nations. What is important is helping teens to understand that they belong somewhere, they have a home, they have people who believe in them, and they are part of a story.

In our family, the most visible form of that message is regular contact with grandparents, aunts, uncles, and cousins. Most of us live far apart, so it can be hard, but with modern technology it's possible to stay close. We've tried to lay a foundation over the years that shows the importance of extended family: calling on birthdays, celebrating holidays together, and making shared summer plans. We have not always been successful; it's easier to maintain some relationships than others. But our sense is that our various efforts have led our teens to understand that their individual stories are part of a larger family story, one we hope they will come to appreciate more and more as they get older.

We have found it a great blessing to include in our family our teens' grandmother, who has lived with us for over a decade. Our observation is that there is something very important about a multi-generational household. Not only is it good for Nana, who is closely involved in day-to-day life and a cherished contributor to our family's well-being, it is also a situation in which our teens have regular interaction with someone whose worldview is entirely different from theirs. To be sure, that can be challenging, as it can sometimes mean there is yet one more person to check in on them and offer suggestions about how to use time other than watching TV or playing with their phones! But more substantially, it allows our teens regular opportunities to understand how their daily experience is not how life always was or how it always will be. They hear stories that take a long view, in contrast to the immediacy and drama of their everyday experiences. Since teens can be isolated within their own little worlds—especially through social media—we believe it is critical that they learn how to interact positively with elders. That learning process can be stressful, but we have no doubt that it will have a positive impact over time.

Pause and Consider

1. How do you connect your teens to a story that is much larger than them? How might you help them have a sense of being part of a longer family story, a larger community?

2. What are some ways that you make time and effort to reach out to extended family or community? What steps might you take to offer your teen the opportunity to know grandparents or other older, wiser figures?

Knowing We Love Them

Consider for a moment the memories of when your teen was a baby or a toddler. What comes to mind?

What are the physical, tactile memories you have of your child—the feel of her skin, the smell of his head after a bath, the warmth of a toddler's hugs? These memories impress themselves on the consciousness of every parent, so it is easy to become nostalgic for those days past.

Less readily memorable are things like changing diapers, cleaning up after messes, enduring days of wailing due to sickness, and so on. We have very selective memories that tend to condense complex periods of our lives. If you are like us, you will recall those time periods with a kind of blissful recollection of a few happy thoughts, sharing a story or two of how adorable your children were at that age.

Take Away

It can be good periodically to revisit old pictures of your teen or to spend time recalling positive experiences. Use those emotions to shape the way you approach interactions with them.

For us, the hard road of experiencing infertility helped make us deeply grateful for the time when we finally did begin raising our children. We took nothing for granted. Everything, from the most banal daily chores to the most intensely bonding experiences with our first child, was a sign of God's grace.

That was many years ago. The novelty, of course, has worn off. But we still try to practice gratitude, especially on important days like birthdays or adoption days. Today, our challenge is different from those early days, based on several factors, including our age and life struggles, our teens' growing independence, and the ordinary ups and downs of life.

The questions that we find ourselves asking are: Do we communicate to our children how much we love them, how much they light up our lives? Do they have a sense of being beloved now, as teenagers, the way they were absolutely sure of it as toddlers? Does our love provide them an anchor in a sometimes-harsh world, a rock amid the shifting sands of school and social life? Do we communicate to our children an unshakable love and acceptance, such that in seeing us they might in some sense intuit the face of God loving them?

There is an interesting short story in the synoptic gospels describing when Jesus was baptized by John in the Jordan River. This is the version from the Gospel of Mark.

> It happened in those days that Jesus came from Nazareth of Galilee and was baptized in the Jordan by John. On coming up out of the water he saw the heavens being torn open and the Spirit, like a dove, descending upon him. And a voice came from the heavens, "You are my beloved Son; with you I am well pleased." (Mk 1:9–11)

The voice from the heavens—the voice of God the Father speaking lovingly to his Son—is striking. Do our teens hear that same confident, proud voice from us? Do they internalize the message "with you I am well pleased"? If we are mindful of our primary job of helping them construct a strong sense of self, then we must be creative in the ways we communicate this fundamental message.

There has been a good deal of research on the dynamics of marital relationships that points to the importance of maintaining a healthy ratio of positive interactions to negative ones: John Gottman, for example, suggests a ratio of 5 to 1.[2] In other words, to build and maintain a healthy relationship with your spouse, you should ideally have at least five positive interactions between you for every one that is less than positive. There is less research on parent-teen interactions, but it stands to reason that a similar logic applies.

It can be easy to find those things we wish our teens did differently and nag them, but it is important to discipline ourselves to find positive ways to interact as well—even to go out of our way, for example, to say something positive. It may be over-the-top to explicitly say "You are my beloved child; with you I am well pleased!"—but we can nevertheless convey that message through praise, words of support or encouragement, or even spontaneous statements that show them how much we like and love them. If our teens hear those positive messages five times more than the critical messages, they will understand that our criticisms are made out of care for who they are becoming.

For Reflection and Conversation

1. Over the past day, what would you guess has been the ratio of positive to negative interactions with your teen? What about over the past week?

2. What are some specific ways you can plan to have positive interactions with your teen?

3. What are some ways that you can make clear to your teen how much you love them?

Loving Them Like God Loves Us

It is telling that the most prominent metaphor for God used in both the Old and New Testaments is that of a parent. Most common is the description of God as a Father, though there are some feminine references to God in both the gospels and the wisdom literature. It is provocative to

imagine God dealing with his people—Israel in the Old
Testament, the Church in the New Testament—the way a
parent deals with his children. We see a similar challenge
of balancing discipline and unconditional love that we
ourselves strive to practice as parents.

For example, in the story of the Garden of Eden, God
arrives after Adam and Eve eat of the fruit they were told
to avoid. God's query to Adam, who is hiding behind
some trees, sounds a lot like the way a parent speaks to an
unruly child: "Did you do the thing I told you not to do?"
Similarly, when Moses comes down from the mountain
to bring his people the Ten Commandments that God has
given him, and he sees them worshiping a golden calf, he
explodes in anger, breaks the tablets of the Law, and storms
away—much like a parent who loses it when a teen acts
defiantly. Again and again we find stories of God and those
who speak for God trying to steer people toward right
choices, only to find that people are stubborn and deter-
mined to make their own choices. Much like adolescents!

What emerges through these stories, though, is a
theme further developed in later stories: God is merciful,
forgiving, and willing to suffer simply to show people
that they are completely beloved. One gets the sense that
Israel's history is not unlike the story of parents and children as they age. There is a wisdom that develops within
the relationship, such that the parents come to a greater
compassion for the children and are willing to accept their
faults, all the while drawing them again and again into
relationship. God's mercy is tenacious, creative, patient,
persevering, and open to change. These are not bad
descriptions of the kind of character traits that parents of
teens must also strive to embody. We must develop habits

of mercy, to "be merciful as your Father is merciful," in the words of Jesus (Lk 6:36). We must develop habits of "mercying"—practicing mercy in our lives as Christians and as parents of teens.

Shortly after being elected pope, Jorge Mario Bergoglio (Pope Francis) selected a motto that would grace all the churches where his papal crest was to be displayed: *miserando atque eligendo,* loosely translated as "mercying and choosing." The motto was a reference to the story of Jesus calling Matthew as his disciple, and it suggests a great image for parents seeking to raise teens to have a discerning faith.

> As Jesus passed on from there, he saw a man named Matthew sitting at the customs post. He said to him, "Follow me." And he got up and followed him.
>
> While he was at table in his house, many tax collectors and sinners came and sat with Jesus and his disciples. The Pharisees saw this and said to his disciples, "Why does your teacher eat with tax collectors and sinners?"
>
> He heard this and said, "Those who are well do not need a physician, but the sick do. Go and learn the meaning of the words, 'I desire mercy, not sacrifice.' I did not come to call the righteous but sinners." (Mt 9:9–13)

Tax collectors were hated for their unjust practices of skimming money off their collections and working for the enemy—imperial Rome—against their own people. So Jesus' choice of Matthew was odd at the very least, and for some, it was scandalous. The Pharisees—those closest to Jesus politically and theologically—represented a more-or-less common opinion among many of Jesus' day: that anyone claiming to speak about God had to be discerning in the choice of company. Then, as now, people believed that your choice of the people you hang with says a lot about you. (Don't we say as much to our kids?)

Jesus' retort is shocking. It's one of many times in the gospels when Jesus comes across as blasphemous, speaking for God in ways that seemed not just presumptuous but close to treasonous to his peers. "I came to call sinners." Who is this "I" that Jesus claims to be? Is he claiming to speak for God? And even if he is—who is he to suggest that God calls sinners? Doesn't God call those who obey the law that he himself gave to Moses—the Ten Commandments and the rest? (Remember "You shall not steal"? Tax collectors steal!)

Here is the answer. Pope Francis chose his motto from a sermon of the Venerable Bede, a historian and theologian of the seventh- and eighth-century Church in England, on the calling of Matthew:

> Jesus, therefore, saw the tax collector, and because he saw by having mercy and by choosing, He said to him, "Follow me." "Follow" means to imitate. "Follow," He said, not so much in the pacing of feet, as in the carrying out of morals. For whoever says that he remains in Christ, ought himself to walk as He walked: which means not striving for earthly things, . . . being advantageous to all, loving, occasioning injuries for no one but patiently suffering those caused to oneself, but seeking always the glory of the Creator, as often as one can raise himself up toward the love of those things which are above.

What Pope Francis wanted to highlight in his choice of "mercying and choosing" as a motto was the way that Jesus showed the compassionate and loving face of God to people who neither deserve nor feel worthy of it. God "mercies" us, Pope Francis suggests, and chooses us. We too must mercy: we must practice the same kind of willingness to forgive our teens "seventy-seven times" in order that they might know our unconditional love for them.

In our lives with our own children, this theme of mercying takes on a number of forms that have become rules for daily life. Here are some examples. Perhaps you have ones that are similar.

1. Pray for your teen without ceasing. Let your model be Saint Monica, whose son was wayward, got a girl pregnant, ran away from home, and later had a profound conversion. We know him today as Saint Augustine.

2. Always end the day by showing your teen some sign of your love: a kiss, a hug, or some other act of affection.

3. Go out of your way to find occasions to praise.

4. Recognize and comment on great choices, especially in times when the teen seems to be making thoughtless choices.

5. Reinforce expectations every day, trying to remain calm. (*Pick up your clothes. Clean up after yourself. Treat others the way you want to be treated.*)

6. Support your teen's efforts whenever possible. Watch games, attend performances, talk to his or her teachers.

7. Show your teen that you not only love but you *like* him or her, in both big and small ways.

These are just a few examples. There are many others. The point is that mercying means fundamentally desiring to become more like Christ ourselves and acting in ways we want our teens to imitate, so that they become more like Christ.

First, mercying means seeing a person as an icon of Christ. The teen is not merely a teen; he or she is a human being, beloved by God, growing every day toward the fully alive human being that he or she will be as an adult. The ancient maxim of Saint Irenaeus may be helpful here: "The glory of God is the human being fully alive." We who love these young people have the potential of seeing them not only as what they are now but also what they eventually will be. What a privilege!

Second, mercying means being fully present to whatever reality the person before me presents, however good or bad. Even while I see the teen as an icon of Christ, I allow myself to see the real person before me, flawed and imperfect yet beautiful. I do not ignore the fact that sometimes this teen makes mistakes, becomes self-focused, hurts me or others I love, or whatever. I see the reality and respond to the reality with love, mindful that the Holy Spirit, too, labors in this growing person to make him or her more fully the person God has created him or her to be.

Not long ago, we were traveling with Kris on college tours while her two siblings stayed home. It was a great chance to reconnect and give her some direct attention. It was also a chance to step out of the normal patterns of communication, which can get bogged down in daily routine and well-worn complaints about doing chores and homework. We resolved that we would do everything possible to maintain positive interactions with her while on the trip, even letting her make decisions about where to eat and how to spend free time. It was good to see her feeling more free and lighthearted; her smile emerged a little more easily than we sometimes see at home. We enjoyed the chance to see her in this carefree way. But after returning home, the old patterns emerged again—thoughtlessness about cleaning up, a desire to withdraw and be alone in her room. Normally, our response would be to scold her. But in light of our trip, and especially in light of coming to feel the weight of a life decision like a college choice, we were more able to sympathize with Kris's situation. We still held her responsible for helping out around the house, but our approach was more focused on building up her sense of self and less on criticizing her being too self-focused.

Perspective Possibilities

Recall an experience when you reacted strongly to something your teen did. As you recall that event, consider how God might see that experience through the eyes of mercy. Is it possible to repeat this practice at other times?

The story of Jesus calling Matthew to become one of his disciples is a story about someone who comes surprisingly into Matthew's life and helps him to take on a new sense of self. When Pope Francis spoke about his new papal motto, he pointed to Caravaggio's painting of the scene, a painting which shows a rather surprised Matthew pointing to himself in response to Jesus' invitation to follow him. His look says, "Who, me?" as if he isn't quite sure he's worthy to respond to Jesus' call. His response is like that of many throughout the Bible: Moses, Jeremiah, Amos, and others who similarly aren't quite sure that they are good or holy enough to serve the Lord. But what is striking about mercying and calling is that it is not about the past; it is about the future. It is not about being an already-healthy person—to use Jesus' metaphor of the physician—but about being a person who will be made healthy by God's grace.

What all this means for us as we parent our teens is that we must balance who they are now and who they will become through love and the gift of faith. This can be difficult at times—we know! Teens are navigating many, many changes in their lives: friends, homework, technology, relationships with adults, hobbies or interests, sex, a sense of meaning, and the list goes on. They are "emerging adults," to use a phrase from educational theory—not yet fully adept at handling all these changes but learning and growing because of them.

For Reflection and Conversation

1. What might be some acts of mercy—underserved, overflowing love like God shows us—that you might plan to show your teen in the next forty-eight hours? The next month?

2. Are there unmet needs in your teen's life that a positive relationship might help?

Seeing the Real Person

We parents have the great privilege of coming to know the unique human beings that God has placed in our lives through birth, adoption, or guardianship. We see these young people as few other people can: their whole selves, with all their gifts and blessings, faults and failings, fears and insecurities, successes and triumphs. We see our teens in their vulnerability, able to sense how they feel in situations both good and bad. Where the world may see a really beautiful woman, we see a girl just starting to have a sense of herself as an adult. Where the world may see a tough-looking guy, we see a boy whose insecurities are masked by an angry mien and new facial hair. The world sees an adult body; we see a growing person.

The story of the disciples seeing Jesus in a new way in the Transfiguration offers parents a clue about what it means to really see our teens as they are, to really know them.

> After six days Jesus took Peter, James, and John his brother, and led them up a high mountain by themselves. And he was transfigured before them; his face shone like the sun and his clothes became white as light. And behold, Moses and Elijah appeared to them, conversing with him. Then Peter said to Jesus in reply, "Lord, it is good that we are here. If you wish, I will make three tents here, one for you, one for Moses, and one for Elijah."
>
> While he was still speaking, behold, a bright cloud cast a shadow over them, then from the cloud came a voice that said, "This is my beloved Son, with whom I am well pleased; listen to him." When the disciples heard this, they fell prostrate and were very much afraid.
>
> But Jesus came and touched them, saying, "Rise, and do not be afraid." And when the disciples raised their eyes, they saw no one else but Jesus alone. (Mt 17:1–8)

The disciples who are closest to Jesus—who have been with him in his ups and downs, times when crowds love him and times when crowds hate him—are privileged to see Jesus in a totally new way. "Lord, it is good that we are here!" Peter remarks, intuiting on a deep level that to see the full reality of Jesus as the Father has revealed him is a unique experience reserved only for those who have been with him through thick and thin.

Jesus himself, after this experience, tells the disciples not to say anything about it to anyone. Perhaps he intuits how little it could mean to those who see him only as a celebrity. Lacking any knowledge about Jesus' inner life and relationship with the Father in prayer, those who hear that God has placed him on a par with Moses and Elijah will only think that he has become conceited and that his followers have been duped.

We are like the disciples: we have seen our teens in their full reality and can say, "It is good to be here." Quite apart from any of the choices that they make, good or bad, we behold them as God says of them, "This is my beloved child, with whom I am well pleased." And God asks us to listen to them. Ours is a privileged view of these emerging adults, whom God invites every day into greater life, greater responsibility, greater love.

Our teens are not always like Jesus, though, and often fall short of the perfect life of God's only Son. It can be difficult on some days to remind ourselves of the full reality of who our teens are. For just as we have the ability to see them in their fullest goodness, we also can see when they make mistakes or hurt others—or even hurt us. We must remind ourselves how hard it can be to have that kind of scrutiny, especially when the magnitude of what teens navigate is so great. Our own discernment process must attend to finding a balance of proclaiming the good and yet not ignoring the bad. At times we've had to navigate some serious moral challenges with Kris, challenges which caused us no small amount of sleeplessness and anxiety. But recalling basic Ignatian principles—like allowing God

to deal directly with the creature, recalling that God has
created Kris for a purpose, and knowing that both the bad
and the good grow like weeds and wheat in every human
heart—has reminded us always to strive to see Kris trans-
figured, a beloved child of God.

Take Away

The word *benediction*, blessing, comes from the Latin meaning "to speak well" of someone. A blessing is an opportunity to speak love to a person. It is a chance to nourish
a person's soul. Be on the hunt for these opportunities in
your teen's life.

Recently, we took the opportunity of Kris's celebration
of the sacrament of Confirmation to write a *palanca*—a
letter of affirmation. The word means "lever" in Spanish,
and developed as a practice, often on Ignatian retreats, of
helping young people to come to a new understanding of
themselves. The palanca "levers" the teen past the hurdle
of a false understanding of self, such as might arise from
negative feedback from peers or unhealthy comparisons to
images in popular culture. The palanca is a straightforward
love letter that says "You are a wonderful person to me,
and here's why." Both Kris's godmother and we wrote separate palancas, emphasizing what we have seen about him
that fills us with joy and gratitude. We shared a little of our
own life journeys, helping Kris to understand life beyond
the limited perspective of sixteen years. We expressed our
hopes, showed sympathy in his struggles, and helped him
understand how much we love him. Here is just a sample:

This letter is a long, loving look at who you are, with a hope that you will come to recognize the difference between "the youest you" and the "you" that other people want you to be. We encourage you to draw your sense of yourself from within. God has created you as a gift to the world and wants you to see yourself as who you truly are, precious and gifted. What we have seen over the past sixteen years—the "youest" you, is the person who is most authentically himself regardless of what other people think of him.

We can still remember how much we were affected by the palancas we received at about the same age. There is something moving about knowing that you are beloved, that you are valuable, and that you have a mission in life. Remember how important it can be to make opportunities to share those messages with your teen.

Ask Yourself

1. What do you see in your teen that others don't see? How might you help your teen understand what you see more deeply?

2. How might you make an opportunity to share a palanca or some other means of communicating what you see in your teen? Is there an opportunity for a retreat or a service project, perhaps connected with a Confirmation or youth ministry program at your parish?

Appreciating Their Gifts

You are the salt of the earth. But if salt loses its taste, with what can it be seasoned? It is no longer good for anything but to be thrown out and trampled underfoot. You are the light of the world. A city set on a mountain cannot be hidden. Nor do they light a lamp

and then put it under a bushel basket; it is set on a
lampstand, where it gives light to all in the house. Just
so, your light must shine before others, that they may
see your good deeds and glorify your heavenly Father.
(Mt 5:13–16)

Jesus preaches these words to the crowds gathered around him on a mountainside as part of what we
now know as the Sermon on the Mount. The sermon as
a whole is a catechism of Christian life, a series of statements describing what it means to repent and believe in
the coming of God's kingdom. Early in his ministry, Jesus
draws followers because of teachings like these, pointing
to the way that God has a particular love for the poor.

This kind of love is as startling today as it was in
Jesus' time. From middle school onward, teens develop
a keen sense of social hierarchy: who's on top, who's on
the bottom, and who's not really even in the hierarchy at
all. Maya van Wagenen, then an eighth grader, wrote a
remarkable memoir about the hierarchy she witnessed at
her middle school. Her book *Popular: Vintage Wisdom for a
Modern Geek* explores her struggles with being at the bottom of the social ladder.[3] She describes trying to move up
the ladder by transgressing social norms—effectively, by
being poised and friendly—often second-guessing whether
she, a "plebeian" is worthy of the kind of social capital
exercised by the "patricians." What she learns over the
course of the book (recommended reading with your middle school daughter!) is how important it is to present her
best self to others, to be authentic, and even to risk rejection
for the sake of establishing new relationships.

Many teens experience a similar self-doubt in the
face of the common social hierarchies they see at school

or among friends. When Kris had to change schools in seventh grade, she became very aware of the kind of hierarchy that Maya describes in her book. As a newcomer, it took time and energy to discern who was most likely to be nice to her, what to wear, and how to act. Much of her energy was spent on how others perceived her. What we hoped she might consider from reading Maya's book was the idea that it was also important to consider how she might become more confident in being herself and less concerned with others' opinions.

Jesus' words above are often read in a "let your light shine" kind of way, as in the song: "This little light of mine, I'm gonna let it shine!" That's certainly a positive message, but it may miss something of what Jesus is getting at, and which suggests something of an edge for teens. Pay attention to the last line: "Your light must shine before others, that they may see your good deeds and glorify your heavenly Father." Jesus connects authenticity with mission. That is, he suggests that being authentic is a reflection of God himself, the one who made us and bestows gifts on us to build up his kingdom. Faithfulness to who we are is faithfulness to God, and is therefore a source of grace.

What does this mean? We remember when our kids were young and full of energy, flinging their arms open to the world and unafraid to sing, play, and dance out of pure joy. As kids get older, they become less spontaneous and more self-conscious, more likely to hide in their rooms and avoid being seen with their parents. On one level, this is perfectly consistent with good developmental psychology. On the other hand, parents need to provide scaffolding that allows our teens to work on the construction of their selves, reminding them that this task is sacred and, if we follow

Jesus' words, an act of worship. They need not recover the same spontaneity they displayed as small children, but we can encourage them that the task of constructing a self is one that God shares with them, laboring with them over time to bring about the kingdom. The task may take years—not unlike earning a degree, writing a novel, making a work of art, or formulating a scientific theory—but the result, the self that each teen is presenting to the world and will present to the world, will give glory to God.

This is good news. "You have a mission!" is our constant message, more often in symbols and gestures than in explicit words. What we hope our teens hear from us is that their lives are not accidents but gifts that God gives to the world. It may take time for them to really understand what those gifts are, particularly if they are not star students, artists, or athletes. Our culture places far too much emphasis on those gifts, which are good but certainly not the only ones that will bring about the kingdom. More important, if we follow Jesus in the Beatitudes, the virtues are oriented towards relationship: being a peacemaker, being pure of heart, being one who seeks justice, and so on. No one earns a varsity letter in peacemaking or is named "best in class" at being pure of heart (even though they should!), but these are lifelong virtues that will continue to grace many lives long after our teens forget what their high school diplomas look like.

Ask Yourself

1. What talents do you see in your teen, even if he or she does not yet see them?

2. What are some interests your teen has expressed— whether at school, or during free time, or while

interacting with others? How might you help cultivate those interests?

3. What are some ways you might expose your teen to new interests? Could you watch a show together, take a trip somewhere interesting, or share a project?

Warts and All

Consider the story of Jesus encountering the Samaritan woman as an example of discernment. In this story from the Gospel of John, Jesus encounters a woman from Samaria—whose inhabitants were intensely disliked by Jesus' fellow citizens—at a well. When Jesus asks her for a drink of water, she expresses surprise, since Jews wanted nothing to do with Samaritans. Jesus draws her into conversation.

> Jesus answered and said to her, "If you knew the gift of God and who is saying to you, 'Give me a drink,' you would have asked him and he would have given you living water."
>
> [The woman] said to him, "Sir, you do not even have a bucket and the well is deep; where then can you get this living water? Are you greater than our father Jacob, who gave us this well and drank from it himself with his children and his flocks?"
>
> Jesus answered and said to her, "Everyone who drinks this water will be thirsty again; but whoever drinks the water I shall give will never thirst; the water I shall give will become in him a spring of water welling up to eternal life."
>
> The woman said to him, "Sir, give me this water, so that I may not be thirsty or have to keep coming here to draw water."

> Jesus said to her, "Go call your husband and come back."
>
> The woman answered and said to him, "I do not have a husband."
>
> Jesus answered her, "You are right in saying, 'I do not have a husband.' For you have had five husbands, and the one you have now is not your husband. What you have said is true."
>
> The woman said to him, "Sir, I can see that you are a prophet. Our ancestors worshiped on this mountain; but you people say that the place to worship is in Jerusalem." (Jn 4:10–19)

This conversation between Jesus and the Samaritan woman is the most detailed story in all the gospels; she is drawn in by Jesus because he is willing to break with social conventions just to be with her. The request for a drink is really nothing more than a pretext for speaking with her; he could have drawn his own water, to be sure, or (more properly) avoided the well altogether, which would have been the right attitude of a Jew in that situation. Jesus just wants to connect with her as a real person, flawed and imperfect, with a message about who God is. The conversation continues:

> Jesus said to her, "Believe me, woman, the hour is coming when you will worship the Father neither on this mountain nor in Jerusalem. You people worship what you do not understand; we worship what we understand, because salvation is from the Jews. But the hour is coming, and is now here, when true worshipers will worship the Father in Spirit and truth; and indeed the Father seeks such people to worship him. God is Spirit, and those who worship him must worship in Spirit and truth."

The woman said to him, "I know that the Messiah is coming, the one called the Anointed; when he comes, he will tell us everything."

Jesus said to her, "I am he, the one who is speaking with you."

At that moment his disciples returned, and were amazed that he was talking with a woman, but still no one said, "What are you looking for?" or "Why are you talking with her?"

The woman left her water jar and went into the town and said to the people, "Come see a man who told me everything I have done. Could he possibly be the Messiah?"

They went out of the town and came to him. . . . Many of the Samaritans of that town began to believe in him because of the word of the woman who testified, "He told me everything I have done." . . . Many more began to believe in him because of his word, and they said to the woman, "We no longer believe because of your word; for we have heard for ourselves, and we know that this is truly the savior of the world." (Jn 4:10–29, 39, 41–42)

Perspective Possibilities

The story of the Samaritan woman at the well is a rich opportunity for prayer. Imagine the scene. Put yourself in the place of the woman and then in the place of Jesus. What do you feel? What do you see?

Jesus speaks with her as she is. His action alone—of breaking social taboos just to spend time with her—is enough to convey the message that she is important. He does not whitewash the fact that she has disregarded God's laws about marriage, but neither does he suggest that her sin is a barrier to their conversation or to his preaching about God. On the contrary: the story is ultimately about how the woman persuades others to meet Jesus because she can speak as one who has been surprised by him. Far from being a hindrance to encountering Jesus, her past—and the shame that likely came from it—made her all the more compelling a witness to him.

In seeing the full reality of who our teens are—in all their beauty and in all their flaws—we seek to see them as Jesus saw the Samaritan woman. Fundamentally, our relationship with them must be rooted in an unequivocal love and acceptance that is evident in actions first, words second. At this stage of their development, talk is still (very) cheap: it will mean nothing unless it grows out of what they witness on a daily basis. Like Jesus, perhaps we need to be a little transgressive in our approach, stepping over the usual boundaries of social propriety to make sure that our teens see our true desire to know them.

One obvious example that comes to mind has to do with social media. Everything we see about teen use of social media, including guidelines from the American Academy of Pediatrics,[4] suggests that we are still in the early stages of understanding the implications of the virtual world that teens create for themselves with almost no adult supervision. Parents of teens need to be more transgressive, to cross over the boundaries that teens themselves create, in order to be present and active in teens' lives. Many parents describe teen years as a time of "withdrawal," in the sense that teens often withdraw from parents and siblings for time by themselves. Now, with more of that time being taken up with social media, our concern is that the otherwise good process of self-reflection that unfolds in solitude can be sidetracked by a hurry-up-and-follow-what's-trending kind of anxiety. Parents need to be transgressive in order to break that pattern and draw teens back into communication.

We have had mixed success with our own efforts. There are strong pressures to stay attached to phones for the sake of group chats, to use one example. At different stages of their growth, our children have been nearly impossible to extract from their devices without a major tantrum. From their perspective, the loss of a phone is exclusion from a social circle, a loss of freedom, and their natural response is to respond in childish ways. We understand that, but we also want to hold them responsible for growing past that childishness in order to develop a more adult sense of balance between the real and virtual worlds.

We understand the need to stay connected to friends and the never-ending cycle of "who's doing what with whom?" Fear of missing out—did you know that FOMO has become an acronym?—has become a significant concern among researchers. According to one study, for example, half of thirteen- to seventeen-year-olds suffer from FOMO anxiety.[5] What we see is the tendency to compare oneself to social media posts, and invariably the emotional takeaway tends to be some sense of inadequacy. Everyone else is more beautiful, everyone else is having a good time, everyone else is connected. Our teens can easily become hyper-aware of their flaws—real or imagined.

Our approach has been two-pronged: First, we hope to limit their exposure to social media in order to limit the likelihood of unhealthy social comparison. Second, we hope to affirm them in their basic goodness, even if only by telling them that they look fine and that how they look is less important than the kind of people they are. It's pretty common during the morning routine to find Kris primping herself in the car mirror, saying something like, "My makeup looks terrible today." Dad's response has commonly become, "Well it's a good thing, then, that you're naturally beautiful." We've begun to wonder whether Kris says something just to elicit that response.

Like Jesus with the Samaritan woman, we want to affirm their basic goodness even if they make poor choices. This can be a delicate balance: it's important to teach them to understand the consequences of actions and, when necessary, to punish them. But in so doing, we want to convey that we love them no less.

Recently, there was a story of a judge who was faced with a case involving a homeless veteran. The vet had clearly broken the law, and so the judge sentenced him to a night in prison. But in this remarkable story, the judge—himself also a veteran—went to the prison and spent the night with him, to show solidarity and compassion even in the face of justice.[6] That image of finding a balance of justice and mercy is helpful in thinking about how we deal with our teens, warts and all. We want to show them a path to justice but walk with them the whole way in order to show them mercy in the process.

For Reflection and Conversation

1. Have you faced a situation of having to discipline your teen? What was that experience like?

2. Do you see your teen wrestling with social comparisons? Does comparing himself/herself to others impact your teen's self-understanding?

3. What limits do you place on social media use or screen
    time? How might you cultivate alternatives to technology use?

4. Are you setting the right example, as a parent, in your
    own use of technology?

Helping Them See the Poor

In Luke's gospel, Jesus begins his public ministry in a synagogue, reading a text from the prophet Isaiah that proclaims God's mercy to the poor:

> The Spirit of the Lord is upon me, because he has
> anointed me to bring glad tidings to the poor. He has
> sent me to proclaim liberty to captives and recovery
> of sight to the blind, to let the oppressed go free, and
> to proclaim a year acceptable to the Lord. (Lk 4:18–19)

This proclamation becomes a major theme throughout Luke's telling of the story of Jesus: he goes out to the margins, healing the sick, spending time among sinners, speaking with lepers, and so on. Here again we see a transgressive approach to those who have internalized shame: Jesus simply wants to connect with them, in order to manifest God's love.

Luke's gospel is the only one of the four canonical gospels in which we find two of the most well-known parables: the Good Samaritan and the Prodigal Son. The story of the Good Samaritan, you'll remember, is the one in which several people pass by a man who has been assaulted and left for dead, but then one person—again, from the hated Samaria (are you seeing a theme here?)— goes out of his way to help the man, paying for his convalescence at a nearby inn. The Prodigal Son story is about a father who runs to embrace his wayward son who had demanded his inheritance early, only to squander it on wine, women, and song. Both of these parables, reflecting Luke's theme of "glad tidings to the poor," are models of how God reaches out, again and again, to find ways to show his people how much he loves them, and how he calls his people to love one another in the same tenacious, extravagant, even embarrassing ways. The father in the story of the Prodigal Son, Jesus says, is like God: he is willing to not only welcome back his wayward son but to literally run out to meet him, in total disregard of any hint of social propriety.

Can you remember examples of loving your teen in embarrassing ways? Of running out to meet them, as it were, after they showed disrespect to you? If so, then you are already intuiting something about "the mind of Christ" (as Saint Paul describes it) in your willingness to humble yourself. You are bringing glad tidings to the poor.

For our teens are indeed poor, in both their understanding of themselves and the world. In some ways they are children in adult bodies, perceived by others as adults while they themselves often feel inadequate and self-conscious. Their internalized shame—born from the barrage of ads reminding them how unattractive they are; friends who slight them; pop culture that lures them through false desires; scowls of adults in authority when they do not perform well; and so many other daily reminders of what they are not—this shame can consume them unless it is balanced by unconditional love.

Parents are the people God sends as ambassadors of his mercy to teens. Often, we alone have the influence, regular contact, oversight, and long view of our teens' lives

that enables us to love them well. Only we can understand
how her part in this play is (for example) a reminder of the
part she didn't get when she was ten; or that this game
against this team is particularly meaningful because of the
awful loss two years ago; or that the grade in this class is
the first A she's ever gotten in math; or that this dance is
a real triumph because of his absolute terror of speaking
to girls.

A number of studies show that the poor give more
than the rich—that the ability to sympathize with others' misfortune makes people more likely to share.[7] There
is something about the experience of shame that carves
out a space in our hearts for others. Teens intuit this on
a deep level: they accept their friends with all their flaws
because they know their own flaws. And while not always
evident—since teens can also become extremely self-focused—many will have a heart for those on the margins
of society: members of racial or ethnic minorities; those
who describe themselves as gay, transgendered, or having other kinds of sexual alterities; the homeless; victims
of human trafficking; and so on. They are likely to draw
cues from the wider cultures that shape them at school or
in social media that point them toward the margins, and
they will discover places in their hearts that move them out
of childish egoism. And while these attempts at expressing
solidarity and generosity of spirit toward others will likely
lack nuance and thorough understanding, it is still important that we acknowledge and appreciate their attempts.

Here is both an opportunity and a challenge. Our vul-
nerable teens will lean more and more on each other and
less on us, their parents. They will perceive the kind of
simple acceptance that their friends provide—willingness

to appreciate them as they are, rather than being reminded constantly of what they are not. In hoping to shape them into adults, our first message must be God's first message of glad tidings to the poor: the Lord loves us wholly, perfectly, unconditionally, quite in spite of our flaws and sins. Only from that foundational message, manifested every day with acts and words of support, can we slowly build in a second message: that so generous are the Lord's gifts to us that God continues to offer them so that we might grow more and more into the very image of God.

The adulthood to which the Lord summons them is not something to be feared—it is a realization of God's gifts, so that their ability to love becomes perfected. All of our reminders throughout the day—*Clean up after yourself; do your homework; be nice to your siblings; put down your phone*, and so on—are really variations of the single message "grow up and accept responsibility." That can be difficult and harsh unless situated within God's invitation to become more and more the person that the Lord has created them to be, to take on a mission that over time will be part of the kingdom God is trying to build in the world. Adulthood is the period of the full flowering of the Lord's gifts to us.

There is another way of looking at Jesus' proclamation that we do well to share with our teens: that God has a special care for poor people and that the way God reaches out to the poor is through his Church. Our hope as parents is that our teens will come to understand that love for the poor means first, not becoming caught up in our selfish desires, and second, developing a consciousness of how we might act in solidarity with the poor. We've already mentioned how the Boston Sock Exchange is one such effort;

so are other volunteer efforts, as well as outreach to those in need in our own community.

For Reflection and Conversation

1. When have you loved your teen in embarrassing ways? Why?

2. Has your teen internalized shame—that is, a sense of not being good enough?

3. What are some ways you might help your teen develop an awareness of the poor and have direct contact with poor people?

4. Are you setting the right example, as parents, for how your family regards those who are less fortunate than you are?

Taking Them to Mass

Our consistent message to our teens, both in deeds and in words, must be an invitation to be part of God's glad tidings to the poor. One specific way that we can manifest that message is to resist the strong tendency to make all life choices based on a calculation of how useful they are: whether in regard to school, sports, friendships, ways of spending time and money, or other arenas. Acts of service and generosity are important, whether towards elderly neighbors, small children, or even friends. But one action we'll focus on is the one that is also what the Catholic Church describes as the source and summit of Christian life: namely, participation in the sacred liturgy.

Your Spiritual Self

What is your attitude toward the Mass? Why do you think Jesus said to his disciples to celebrate the Eucharist "in memory of me"? Do you see a connection between the Mass and Jesus' constant call to pay attention to the poor?

We use the somewhat formal term "sacred liturgy" to refer primarily to the Mass (the Eucharist), as well as other celebrations throughout the Church's year. We are convinced that there is no substitute for regular participation in Mass over the course of a child's life. No religious education program, no retreat, no service program, no book or digital resource can substitute for regular worship. We have seen many variations on the theme over our years of ministry and teaching: occasional Mass-going with some regular participation in religious education, religious education without Mass, participation in Mass only with extended family on holidays, and so on. What we see, though, among teens who have an active faith, are stories of Mass being a weekly (or more frequent) practice. From that practice there develop many other connections with the Church and its traditions. Teens gain a network of friends who reinforce faith (what sociologists might call *plausibility structures*) and help them develop practices of discernment through imitation. They develop a deeper religious vocabulary and conceptual framework which allows them to have a place to "stand" when looking at the world and trying to make sense of hard questions, like those that deal with suffering, evil, love, and hope. Most importantly, they develop the habit of considering the Eucharist—Christ sacramentally present to us—as the focal point of their spiritual lives, along with everyone else they come to know through the regular practice of their faith. They develop a faith that is not fundamentally about themselves but about Christ and those called to serve Christ's kingdom.

Participation in the liturgy is a reminder that, as Catholics, we regard these celebrations as more than just rituals or services. They are ways that we participate in a particularly visible way in the mystical Body of Christ alive in human history. There is no more important way that we train our teens in developing a discerning approach to life than by regular practice of celebrating liturgy. The sacred liturgy is a practice of "dwelling in the house of the Lord," the place where the Lord invites the poor, the outcast, the suffering, and the marginalized to his banquet.[8]

The word *liturgy* comes from the Greek word for worship, but etymologically, the word can be rendered "the work of the people." Inviting children at an early age to regular participation in this work becomes habit by the time they are teens, but even teens who begin the practice anew have the opportunity, with the right guidance, to see it as the way that, as a Church, we invite a piece of heaven into the world. How? By directing our words, actions, song, visual art and architecture, and community participation toward God. By placing our life's struggles, our attempts at generosity, our hopes for perfection, our laments about sin and evil before the Lord. By picking up our crosses and following Christ in the midst of life's joys and life's hardships. By joining together with the very old; the very young; the rich; the poor; the healthy and sick; the black, white, and brown; the male and female across the world to remember and celebrate God with us. By sharing the Body and Blood of Christ in his memory, the liturgy is a summons to become our best selves in a world that often wants to drag us, slouching, toward lesser selves. Even when liturgy is done poorly, it is a striving towards beauty, and beauty is the ultimate resistance against the many ways the world entices teens to consume their way to unhappiness. Beauty—if we teach them to behold it, for it can be obscured by false desires—exists for its own sake as a window to God.

We don't want to suggest that every experience of Mass is easy for teens or that we never have arguments about having to go every week. Our kids complain from time to time, but even so, they have come to understand that this is an expected part of every Sunday. We've started developing practices around the Mass that contribute to making it a positive experience, such as going out for breakfast together afterwards or connecting with friends who are also there. The important point we're making is less about making sure our kids get to Mass, as if to check off an item on a weekly to-do list, and more about ensuring that their understanding of God, of the ministry of Christ, of the teaching of the Church, about people, and about themselves is shaped by participation in liturgy. Recalling the stress on imagination we see in Ignatian spirituality, we hope that the Mass provides an imaginative space—enhanced by stained glass windows, beautiful music, the presence of different types of people, and liturgical actions of praise, thanksgiving, lament, contrition, peace offering, and reception of the Eucharist—during which our teens imagine themselves as being part of Christ's mission in the world.

From the liturgy we learn and practice being "sent" (*missa* in Latin, from which we get the word *Mass*) into the world to build the kingdom of God. "Earth's crammed with heaven," wrote Elizabeth Barrett Browning, suggesting that the whole world is a place of encountering God for those who have developed eyes to see. To be sure, developing these eyes takes more than mindless mumbling of prayers week after week. One of the teens we surveyed expressed it well: she had fallen into routine, but once her life was "thrown into a whirlwind" (her words), she found that the liturgy centered her and gave her a language with which to reach out to God in her distress. She had become poor but discovered in that experience that the Lord does indeed bring glad tidings to the poor.

Pause and Consider

1. Is going to Mass a priority in your family? Why or why not?

2. Have you given your teen opportunities to experience really good liturgy—for example, a Christmas or Easter vigil, or a Mass at a basilica or cathedral?

Chapter Four

Freedom to Become Their Best Selves

Today you are You, that is truer than true.
There is no one alive who is Youer than You.

DR. SEUSS, *HAPPY BIRTHDAY TO YOU!*

For me to be a saint means to be myself. Therefore the problem of sanctity and salvation is in fact the problem of finding out who I am and of discovering my true self.

THOMAS MERTON, *NEW SEEDS OF CONTEMPLATION*

It can be wonderful to watch our teens begin to inhabit more adult roles and grow in their talents and abilities. Whether we are seeing a play in which a son or daughter shows great poise, or a game in which he or she excels, or an opportunity for public speaking—these can be opportunities to see our teens grow in freedom. As parents, we have a particular way of understanding the long roads that they travel to become good at something, and we can rejoice at seeing the glimpses of them getting there.

Take Away

Resist the temptation to think your teen has to have a passion and be great at something. That language is too often caught up in unhealthy forms of competition. Ask yourself instead when you have seen the most real version of your teen. Have you let him or her know how much you love that realest self?

We pointed earlier to the difference between autonomy and freedom. Now, let's expand on how we consider helping teens grow in freedom. Here, we will point to the rich notion of freedom that emerges from a biblical understanding of the person as created by God to do some good in the world.

Consider several images: the freedom of a shortstop whose skills in defense have been honed over many years; the ballet dancer whose freedom in dance is the fruit of many years of practice; the singer who progressed through learning scales to understanding complex forms of modern music; the doctor who spent years in college and medical school studying text after text and putting in hundreds of hours in clinical rotations. In every case, the freedom that comes from being excellent at something is the direct fruit of being tutored by those who have gone before. One submits to the wisdom of the past, knowing that over time, it releases a person to develop new expressions of excellence. One's freedom is the fruit of discipline.

The spiritual life is no different. By submitting ourselves to the wisdom of our faith tradition, we develop a kind of excellence in the spiritual life. We come to deeper understanding of Jesus through attention to the scriptures and grow in relationship to Jesus through communion with the Church, particularly by the repeated experience of attending Mass and participating in the sacraments. By guiding our teens through growth in that relationship, we hope that they, too, may discover their freedom.

Yet in the Ignatian tradition, there is an even more fundamental understanding of why it is possible for us to reach for freedom, in light of the fact that our desires often lead us away from the life God invites us to live. In several places throughout his letters, Saint Paul describes how Christ has set us free from sin and given us a new relationship with God the Father. "For freedom Christ has set us free; so stand firm and do not submit again to the yoke of slavery," he writes in the letter to the church in Galatia (Gal 5:1). Paul reflects on his early experience of being faithful to the law of Moses, but he becomes so zealous for that law that he persecutes the followers of Christ, hunting and killing them. Only after a profound conversion does he repent of his earlier life and come to a new understanding of the freedom that Christ offers him.

> [But] whatever gains I had, these I have come to consider a loss because of Christ. More than that, I even consider everything as a loss because of the supreme good of knowing Christ Jesus my Lord. (Phil 3:7–8)

Paul comes to understand freedom as a gift of God's grace, which interrupts his former life and steers him toward a whole new purpose.

In many places, Paul reflects on the paradox of freedom: it always comes at a price. We always end up following someone or something. In his case, the freedom of being a "slave of Christ" (1 Cor 7:22) is vastly superior to being a slave of something that is not God (Gal 4:8). We have, according to Paul, been "purchased at a price" by Christ (1 Cor 6:20)—set free from slavery to that which is not God and which leads us away from God.

Freedom is the gift that God offers every human being. As parents, we do well to reflect on this gift. What does it mean to be free? Our usual answer will probably reflect some understanding of the political freedoms we enjoy: freedoms of speech, religion, the press, voting, and so on. Those are important things that are good to teach to young people. But more important, and more consequential to the ways we choose to live, is an understanding of freedom as a fundamental capacity to choose how to respond to any situation.

Such was the understanding of Viktor Frankl, a psychologist and Nazi concentration camp survivor who reflected on the different ways that people responded to the horrors of camp life. For Frankl, the most fundamental of human freedoms—the one that remains even when every other element of a person's life has been stripped away—is the way he or she chooses to respond.[1]

From an early age, parents intuit something of what Frankl points to. We want our children to develop capacities for making good choices so that they will neither rely on their parents all the time nor blindly follow their friends or what they see on TV. We want them to develop a strong sense of themselves and their abilities. We prod them to make good choices about diet, exercise, screen time, reading, responsibilities, and so on. As they get older, we encourage them to make good choices about homework, recreation, drug and alcohol use, sex, jobs, and relationships. We seek a balance between lecturing them and leaving them entirely on their own. That balance-seeking is itself a significant part of our own discernment process as parents.

Remember how we cultivate our own discernment, as well as help our teens grow in discernment as discussed in chapter 2. Rooted in a faith in God, and a faith that God has created us to do some good in the world, discernment aims toward deepening our understanding of who God is and who God has created us to be. The same is true for both our own spiritual lives and the growing spiritual lives of our teens.

Our focus is on our teens' growing autonomy and our hope that they will grow in freedom, understood as living fully into the kinds of persons God has created them to be. Freedom, in this rich theological sense, is nothing less than an embrace of that creation: a desire to be who God has made me to be, discerned through careful listening to the voice of God.

Do you remember what you wanted to do with your life when you were, say, fourteen? We were mindful of this question when we were talking recently with Kris about school work and thinking about college. Both of us can recall the kinds of ways we imagined our lives might unfold, and having conversations with our parents about what we would do when we grew up. Suffice it to say that sometimes those conversations started with complaints about too much homework! Remembering that point, our conversation with Kris was an attempt to propose things for him to imagine so that he might develop motivation to work hard in school. If you're like us, you've probably had moments when you've had to push back against a more-or-less carefree, have-fun attitude. The naively autonomous teen may want to avoid work (as, at times when we were their age, we did)—but the teen who grows into the freedom of knowing that he has talents and gifts to offer the world will want to work toward realizing them.

We've begun to see the fruits of this nascent kind of freedom in our teens. When once there was pushback against doing homework, now more often we see diligence from someone preparing to take the SAT test. When once there was shyness and reticence in meeting new people, now we see someone who has transitioned to a new school and made friends with a terrific group of people. When once there was anger and frustration at losing (any kind of game or competition), now we see a growing sense of sportsmanship and enjoyment of shared play. These small steps in growing freedom are, we hope, the beginning of a lifetime of growing more and more into the persons that God has created our children to become.

Note that we are describing freedom here in primarily moral terms: that is, in ways that describe the actions and habits that shape them as human beings in everyday life. More complex is the specific question of religious faith, which unfolds (we believe) on a different timetable. All people must make concrete choices, and so we hope to influence the kinds of choices our teens make. But the choice of practicing a living faith is different. Our hope is that ultimately their choice to grow in moral freedom moves in harmony with their choice to practice a living religious faith; but we also want to recognize that the two do not always unfold together.

Ask Yourself

1. Can you identify with what Saint Paul means by freedom? Would you describe your relationship with God as one that has set you free (to know the truth, to love others, to reject a sinful past, or something else)?

2. Do you consider faith something that will enable your teen to become more free?

3. Do you hope that your teen practices Christian faith in contrast to other ways of living today?

What Is Most Important in Life?

The archetypal story of faith in the Bible is that of Abraham, called by God to leave his homeland in order to travel to a land that God has promised him (Gn 12:1). What makes the story so fundamental is that it is a story about moving from a place of comfort to an unknown place, a place I have never been but a place where God will reveal his promises to me.

The story is equally relevant for parents and for teens. For many of us, family life during the childhood years brings images of play, the rhythms of learning and sharing time together, holidays, milestones like losing a tooth or learning to read, and so on. While no families are the same, and while no families are perfect, still there are key guideposts to the developmental stages proper to families with younger children. But as children become teens, the script changes, and often quite dramatically. Former patterns of relationship are now awkward or embarrassing.

Prior ways of celebrating or spending time together now feel outdated. Often, teens prefer being with friends than with family. In sum, both parents and teens have left a place of comfort and entered an unknown place.

In that unknown place, we have found it important to search for new ways of establishing trust. Sometimes we fail, but with persistence our hope is that our teens will still understand what we are trying to teach them. One important example is about how to live in this new unknown place: how to find their way, whom to trust, what to hope for, and what to work toward. *Don't be afraid to grow up*, we say in a hundred different ways, not so much with explicit words as with how we are supporting them.

For example, our teen Kris can be confusing sometimes: she wants to be left alone, but then she'll come and ask Dad to pick her up like a child. She shows responsibility at work, but then comes home and refuses to do any chores. She makes attempts to do cooking on her own, but then has tantrums because her parents didn't do her laundry. These and many other examples over the normal course of daily life suggest that Kris is negotiating a fundamental question: Do I want to grow up? Do I want to have greater autonomy, or do I like the fact that my parents do things for me?

As we have come to understand how Kris negotiates this question about growing up, we have asked ourselves a related question: Are we showing Kris that it's good to be a grownup? Or are we more likely to appear burdened by our adult lives?

Let's face it: life can be hard. Bills, work, family responsibilities, home upkeep, giving time to kids, planning for the future, filing taxes, shopping—all these tasks can add to our daily stress level. By contrast, what Kris sees on TV, in movies, in popular music, online, and in the world she inhabits are examples of carefree rich kids who do whatever they want. We've become really angry at portrayals of parents and other adults on most kids' and teens' shows, for example—most are bumbling idiots or vicious lunatics. The not-so-subtle message they hear reinforced in pop culture is *stay young; it's more fun.* Of course that culture is fueled by advertisers who cater to adolescent desires.[2] It's no surprise that, according to the US Census, more and more adults are deliberately choosing to avoid ever having kids at all.

We decided that it was important to model for Kris that adulthood, while a time of responsibility for many things, is nevertheless a time of great freedom, of living into the richness of relationships and coming to deeper knowledge of what is most meaningful in life. At one point, reflecting on stories of celebrities and politicians who cheated on their spouses, Kris opined that there was really no such thing as love. Incredulous, we pointed out that we were committed to our marriage and would never lose that relationship. "Yeah, but you have that third thing," she observed dismissively. "You know . . . *God.*" (Inside, we were doing the happy dance.) Evidently, Kris had recognized that faith in God made all the difference: we had conveyed that living together rooted in a shared faith led us to freedom and happiness in our marriage.[3]

Consider this question of freedom as you read Jesus' words about the kingdom of heaven:

> The kingdom of heaven is like a treasure buried in
> a field, which a person finds and hides again, and
> out of joy goes and sells all that he has and buys that

field. Again, the kingdom of heaven is like a merchant searching for fine pearls. When he finds a pearl of great price, he goes and sells all that he has and buys it. (Mt 13:44–46)

Jesus points to the kingdom as the fulfillment of what we most earnestly desire out of life. The kingdom is a treasure or a "pearl of great price"—it's something that a person will give up everything to have. That's certainly what Saint Paul thought when he reflected on his life before and after coming to know Jesus—remember that he calls knowing Jesus the "supreme good."

The message that we hope to communicate to Kris is that growing up is an invitation to grow in both autonomy and freedom. Yes, we say, you'll be able to drive places on your own. Yes, you'll make money and choose how to spend it. Yes, you'll develop relationships and maybe even fall in love with someone. All these things are good.

At the same time, we hope to communicate that autonomy is also the means to greater freedom. By making decisions about your life, we want Kris to understand, you must recognize the great gift of responsibility: the ability to choose actions rooted in love that ultimately move us in the direction of the pearl of great price. Autonomy that leads to selfishness is a dead end, but autonomy that leads to responsibility leads to greater and greater freedom.

For Reflection and Conversation

1. What does your teen think is the most important truth in life? What does he/she hope for out of life?

2. Do you see evidence of your teen thinking about the future and what he/she wants to do with it?

3. Who are the people—heroes or heroines—to whom you want your teen to be introduced? Are there saints, artists, or leaders whom you hope might inspire your teen? How might you introduce them?

Which Desires Are Authentic?

The theorist and literary critic René Girard has suggested that from an early age we learn to desire what we see others desiring. Toddlers want the toy that they see another toddler playing with. Children want to do the things they see their friends doing. Teens want the same clothes, devices, and experiences that they see their peers and role models enjoying. Even as adults, our desires are shaped to a great extent by our peers. The point is that this fundamental pattern is not always good for us, and so we must develop habits that allow us to discern which desires are authentic, rooted in hearts open to becoming the persons God has created us to be.

The saints intuit this basic truth. They come to understand that ordinary patterns of life are often marked by attitudes which do not serve the kingdom. To use a broad example, the usual understanding of "the American dream" may reflect a naïve attitude toward consuming things, prioritizing status over relationships, or ignoring biases toward those who don't fit our idea of what it means to be American. Saints work with the poor; they reach out to those on the margins; they eschew wealth and other markers of success; they challenge our political categories and, like Jesus, hang out with unsavory characters.

For teens, the pattern identified by Girard may lead them to desire all sorts of things which lead to harm: drug or alcohol use, eating disorders, sexual behavior, self-harm, and so on. We've noticed an unfortunate pattern among several young TV and movie stars, for example—kids who start with an everybody's-next-door-neighbor persona but who, as they get older, start getting into self-destructive behaviors. They may unconsciously internalize common values, lacking the ability to see a bigger picture or a sense of how their choices today impact the kinds of people they become tomorrow.

One exercise that Tim has used in class to challenge these patterns is for students to answer the question, "What will you, as parents, advise your children to do?" In our own household, we've seen Kris sometimes offer spontaneous observations about what to do as a parent. Surprisingly, that parenting style can sometimes seem very harsh! Clearly, Kris has some awareness of how choices as a teen may not always take into account the larger questions of how to flourish over a lifetime. It can be good to prompt teens to consider this larger picture.

Jesus himself shows an awareness of our tendencies to stress over things we think we want.

> Therefore I tell you, do not worry about your life, what you will eat [or drink], or about your body, what you will wear. Is not life more than food and the body more than clothing? Look at the birds in the sky; they do not sow or reap, they gather nothing into barns, yet your heavenly Father feeds them. Are not you more important than they? Can any of you by worrying add a single moment to your life-span? Why are you anxious about clothes? Learn from the way the wild flowers grow. They do not work or spin. But I tell you that not even Solomon in all his splendor was clothed like one of them. If God so clothes the grass of the field, which grows today and is thrown into the oven tomorrow,

will he not much more provide for you, O you of little
faith? (Mt 6:25–30)

How many times have you told your teen, "Don't
worry about your body! It's fine the way it is!" or "Your
clothes look just fine as they are!"? Teens are naturally concerned about their appearance because they understand
that it is an important dimension of a person's social capital. We may want to tell them that appearance isn't everything, but they see the way we dress for work or for going
out and recognize that we too value it. Jesus' message to
all of us, though, is that in the big picture, it is important
to first seek the kingdom.

Your Spiritual Self

Don't worry if you don't consider yourself particularly
religious. The point is not to measure ourselves according to some external standard of piety. It's fundamentally
about developing a friendship with God. Start today—just
talk to God, or rely on a prayer like the Our Father.

It is important to remember as parents that our influence
is greater than we may think. Teens will push back against
what they perceive to be their parents' out-of-touch ways,
but research shows that they will still, for the most part,
take our words seriously.[4] If we model for them that our
own lives are fundamentally dependent on God, over time
that message will sink in. That means seeing us pray, reading the Bible, talking about faith openly, reaching out to
others in service, regularly giving money to the Church
and to the poor—these and other regular *concrete practices*
that show us committed to growing in relation to God.

That doesn't mean we will see the fruits of that message right away—especially since it is common today for teens and young adults to withdraw from religious practices and beliefs. But what we have seen is that the way parents manifest their faith, especially through regular participation in liturgy, has an impact on teens' worldview nonetheless. While they may not consider themselves Catholic (for however long), many will, for example, report sharing fundamental beliefs about, for instance, the dignity of the poor, the need to work toward a good society, the reality of love, and the possibility for good deeds to make a real difference. We have seen how these foundational beliefs can be like soil in which seeds of faith bloom as young people mature into adults.

Pause and Consider

1. In what ways do you see your teen too easily going along with the crowd?

2. What is the evidence that your teen will see that your life is built primarily on depending on God? How do you model faith?

Helping Their Faith Take Root

Jesus' Parable of the Sower is essential for parents, especially those with teens who may show difficulty or unwillingness to embrace the faith we hope to share with them.[5]

> [Jesus said,] "Listen! A sower went out to sow. And as he sowed, some seeds fell on the path, and the birds came and ate them up. Other seeds fell on rocky ground, where they did not have much soil, and they sprang up quickly, since they had no depth of soil. But when the sun rose, they were scorched; and since

they had no root, they withered away. Other seeds fell
among thorns, and the thorns grew up and choked
them. Other seeds fell on good soil and brought forth
grain, some a hundredfold, some sixty, some thirty. Let
anyone with ears listen!" (Mt 13:3–9)

Jesus compares the seeds to the word of God which takes
root in some people's hearts but not in others. For many
parents, it is a source of great stress to see that some of their
teens refuse to practice their faith, while others marvel at
how faith takes root and brings forth great acts of love.

The parable hints at what is happening. Jesus points
to the freedom of every human being—God does not force
the seeds of his word into anyone's heart. Rather, he scat-
ters it widely, liberally, prodigally, hoping that people will
respond in freedom by providing a hospitable place for it
to grow. For some, there are too many factors in their world
which carry away the word. The birds which eat the seed
may be teens' overwhelming need to fit into the crowd, or
traumas in their lives, or unformed senses of themselves.
For others, the youthful embrace of faith that they might
have showed at a summer camp or volunteer opportunity
has no depth because it goes unnourished by the rich soil
of a community that reinforces what they believe on a daily
basis. Their faith becomes starved and it withers away
as they mature intellectually but not spiritually. For still
others, faith is strangled by a community that disparages
faith and the need to belong overwhelms a still nascent
faith until it becomes only a memory.

There are others who receive the word and let it
grow in them to become transformative. We've known
teens whose faith has led them to do wonderful things—
beautiful acts of self-giving that manifest a whole-hearted

response to God. They become leaders among their peers and their fruitfulness can help enrich the soil of other teens' lives. It is good for parishes and pastoral leaders to offer teens opportunity for such leadership.

We've seen a number of examples of the ways that teen leadership can benefit a parish, school, or diocese. Anyone who has been to a World Youth Day (WYD), for example, knows how electric the atmosphere can be when young people are given the chance to express their faith together. We've led groups to this event as well as other local events that focus on worship or service. While WYD or events like the Steubenville conferences can be powerful, they are not for everyone: they require careful preparation, and teens themselves can be the ones to help organize group meetings. Both of us had such opportunities in our teens, and our hope that our teens will take advantage of them too. We've seen teens who have developed confidence in their leadership skills as a result of helping lead a service project or a prayer gathering, and who have gone on to be leaders on their college campuses or, in a few cases, even as professionals in various forms of ministry or service.

One example that we witnessed in our parish was a Lenten service led entirely by teens. It was a meditation on the Passion during the Triduum, and it involved reading the gospel story, sharing images on a screen, and music. It was a beautiful meditation, made even more beautiful by the fact that they had put a good deal of effort into it. Another example, from a number of years ago when Sue was a youth minister, was her effort to draw teens into leadership positions as part of a new Life Teen program. For several, the opportunity to take on leadership roles was the first time an adult had asked them for help in undertaking something new.

As professionals, we've seen great examples of teens in whom the seed of God's word has taken root, and been inspired by their faith. But as parents, the question is very different. The critical question for us now is how to help cultivate the soil so that our teens might be receptive to God's word. First, though, let's clarify what "God's word" means here—that is, what it means to help our teens develop a living faith.

First, it means moving them away from selfishness to awareness of others. More than anything else, it means working tirelessly to help them understand that they are not the center of the world—a common default setting for early adolescents and children. For many parents, this is really a task that can last for years. It's often our own fault—we praised them so much, and for the tiniest things, when they were little! There is no easy recipe for how to do this, but introducing them early and often to work that involves other people is certainly important. It may be necessary to seek out youth groups, camps, or volunteer opportunities—anything that gets them out of the normal dynamics of herd mentality.

Second, it means giving them opportunities to understand their giftedness to others. Teaching them skills such as cooking, making crafts, playing music, creating art, writing, playing sports, or any number of other activities can put them in positions that elicit praise and gratitude from others. Helping them understand that these gifts, talents, and capacities with which God has endowed them can be used for the good of others as well as themselves can give them a window to their expanding freedom.

Third, it means sharing with them the experience of worship. We are suggesting this in an expansive, rather than narrow, sense. Worship is not only about going to church, which as we've said is more than good, it is essential; but rather, this is about orienting our lives fully towards God. Going to church ought to be one significant manifestation of our worship, but for it to be real it must encompass our entire lives. Do our teens see that our lives are oriented toward God, or do they see church as an add-on to our lives on weekends or holidays? Do they understand that all our relationships, professional aspirations, uses of money and time, and priorities all have to do with what God calls us to do with our lives?

Fourth, sharing God's word with teens will mean that we make regular, consistent efforts to connect our shared worship with reflective discernment on what it means in our lives. Here, again, we return to our Ignatian toolbox. We need to help them understand scripture and the stories of the Church and her saints. We should give them religious education and celebrate the sacraments. We must make regular participation in the Eucharist a priority, and model the importance of practicing forgiveness and celebrating the sacrament of Reconciliation. We need to share with them different ways of praying and help them to understand the spiritual life. We should make explicit connections between our faith tradition and key moral questions, especially those that impact their lives directly as teens. We should educate ourselves and them in the rich theological and spiritual traditions of the Church. In short, we need to help them understand what it means to "inhabit" the life of faith and how it is a foundation for our own freedom as adults.

In sum, cultivating the soil of our teens' faith is most importantly cultivating our own faith and living it out as parents. For if we live in "the freedom of the children of God" ourselves, naturally the joy of that freedom will spill over into a desire to share it with those we love.

Even if we do this in faith, Jesus' parable reminds us that ultimately our teens too have freedom and will encounter God's word in the concrete circumstances of their life journeys. The soil may be rocky or thorny right now, but over time it may become softened through our prayers. As parents we can never give up on our teens, even if there are times in their lives when they may find it easy to give up on themselves.

Our model as parents is Saint Monica, the mother of Saint Augustine, who prayed earnestly for her son through many years of heartache, which included robbery, sexual indiscretions, life in a gang, and participation in marginal religious and political movements—until finally the Lord caught up with him and softened his heart so that it might bring forth great fruit.

Pause and Consider

1. What experiences might help your teen develop a spirit of generosity towards others?

2. Are there parents you know whose grown children are examples of a well cultivated faith? Can you talk to them about what resources might be helpful for cultivating your teen's faith?

3. Do you pray for your teen? Do you share with him or her the things you are praying about?

How to Be Happy

Of all the answers to the question "What do you hope your child will be when he or she grows up?" the best one we've heard is "Unbelievably happy." It's common for parents to project our hopes onto our children—we want them to be doctors or lawyers or engineers, stars in whatever they do, king or queen of the homecoming parade. Those can be good for some people. But through the eyes of faith, a world of possibilities opens up for our teens so they need not be herded toward the same goals as everyone else. Our job, in helping them to become free, must involve helping them consider a broad understanding of their happiness that is not limited to the usual paths of success.

Toward Health and Holiness

In an epic seventy-five-year study of Harvard men, researchers found that of all the usual markers of success, the one that ultimately proved to be the key to happiness was strong relationships, which impacted both physical health and mental health. How might we teach our teens to practice the virtues of good relationships?

We were recently on a mission trip that involved a visit to the US–Mexico border in Nogales. There, we participated in an effort to offer food and guidance to migrants, many of whom had been fleeing crushing violence or dire poverty. We met a young woman there who worked full-time for the organization that sponsored the effort and were deeply impressed by her commitment. She told her story of having first encountered this work as a volunteer in college and having then chosen a college major rooted in the desire to do the work full-time. She learned Spanish and discovered a desire to serve displaced people.

We wondered what enabled her to discover this desire. So much of what teens see around them, from entertainment to sports to politics to the usual high school dramas, can be rooted in various forms of selfish desire. On top of that, they are immersed in cultures of relentless competition: on the athletic field, in the classroom, in college preparation, in seeking internships and even volunteer opportunities. Over and over we teach young people—either deliberately or unconsciously—to fend for themselves and beat out their peers.

In our family, we try mightily to not get too caught up in competition. Sometimes it can be good: it can sometimes bring out our best. But what we really hope our teens discover is that real happiness comes from the discovery of how God calls us to give of ourselves. "Whoever wishes to save his life will lose it, but whoever loses his life for my sake will find it," Jesus says (Mt 16:25). Sometimes we can forget how radical a claim this is, particularly for young people whose lives are still before them. Why not seek a prestigious school and a lucrative career? Why not try as hard as possible to land the best internship? Why not do everything possible to work the system and get the best grade point average? Why not choose a university based on how likely they are to win a major national championship, or how high they are ranked?

The answer, we have become convinced, is that external measures of success, while initially satisfying, are simply not good measures of what will bring us freedom or happiness in our lives. External measures of success

represent ways in which people shoehorn their desires
into whatever others desire, and are thus rooted in an
unformed sense of self. They can be rooted in a kind of
anxiety, inasmuch as we want to make life choices that
will secure us what appear to be necessary elements of
happiness like income and health. A young person may
have a beautiful gift for making pottery, for example, but
judge that this talent is simply not going to enable him
to make a living. Seeing that investment bankers make
good money, and being a good student, our young potter
may simply go after the finance degree and leave pottery
making behind. But what that young person may miss are
the struggles and creativity that might, over time, have led
him to leverage his artistic skill into a career that benefits
not only himself, but others.[6]

Jesus' recipe for happiness is outlined in his well-
known Sermon on the Mount. In particular, the statements
that have come to be known as "Beatitudes" (from the
Latin word *beatus*, meaning happy) are disarming statements that are pretty much the opposite of what most
people would consider the way to be happy. According
to Jesus, the happy (or "blessed") are the poor, sad, meek,
just, and merciful, as well as peacemakers and those who
are persecuted for believing in him. Try telling *that* to your
teen!

The only way to understand what Jesus is saying
about happiness, and to help your teen to consider it, is to
remember what he says about the kingdom of heaven: it's
ultimately about falling in love. When our hearts are fixed
on an irreplaceable good—that is, a good that *we know we
are made for*, then we are willing to go exactly where Jesus
says we are blessed.

Think about happiness in terms of your parenting. Doesn't being a parent mean signing up for the Beatitudes?

1. You are poorer than you would be without kids.

2. You share the sadness of all the trials and tribulations your teens face. You feel it when they get a bad grade or are mistreated by a peer.

3. You know meekness: pleading with a teacher or coach on your teen's behalf.

4. You viscerally feel it when someone treats your teen unjustly.

5. You practice mercy with your teen all the time: choosing to overlook daily annoyances; giving multiple chances after they screw up; constantly helping them make good choices.

5. You are a peacemaker between your kids when they fight or when your teen complains about someone else.

6. You take a lot of heat for insisting that your teen go to Mass.

The Beatitudes are statements about what being in love looks like. They are also statements about what freedom looks like. Notice that neither love nor freedom means perfect bliss at all moments. For that, we must wait for heaven. But love and freedom do mean that we are living as God has made us capable of living, helping to build the kingdom. And our task is to help our teens be willing to do the same.

For Reflection and Conversation

1. How might you find opportunities to share with your
   teen the source of your happiness? Even if you are
   going through a hard time, how might you communicate what keeps you going?

2. Has your teen ever asked you about married life, or
   about work life, or something else that amounts to fish-
   ing for what makes life happy? How did you respond?

What Do You Want?

To help our teens learn what is worth loving, we must ask
them to pay careful attention to their desires. There are
always two questions we can ask them:

1. What do you want?
2. What do you really want?

As parents, we have a pretty good sense of how our
teens will answer the first question. They will have variations on basic themes: they want to be popular, they want
money or success, they want to get good grades, they want
clothes and iPhones and video games, and so on. In our
experience, teens are able to name surface desires, but are
also perfectly capable of recognizing *that* they are surface
desires. We must be vigilant to create or discover opportunities when they can identify real desires, desires which
point them toward discovery of themselves as created by
God to do some good in the world. We must help them be
willing to fall in love.

What does this mean? Pedro Arrupe, the former superior general of the Jesuits, exhorted people to discover

something about who God created them to be by being willing to fall in love.

> Nothing is more practical than finding God, that is, than falling in love in a quite absolute, final way. What you are in love with, what seizes your imagination, will affect everything. It will decide what will get you out of bed in the morning, what you will do with your evenings, how you will spend your weekends, what you read, who you know, what breaks your heart, and what amazes you with joy and gratitude. Fall in love, stay in love and it will decide everything.[7]

What we learn from Ignatian spiritual practices is developing "eyes to see," as Jesus called them, eyes that can find beauty in places where some people don't look, like on the side of the road where a man may have been beaten by robbers or in the pleading eyes of ten lepers. Having eyes to see means discovering sources of desire that surprise us, and suggest to us that God is moving our hearts toward a purpose for which he has created us.

A clue to how falling in love might happen is when we see our teens identifying an interest outside the norms of what their friends are doing. We shared one example earlier, when Kris first tried out working at the Boston Sock Exchange. We must be willing to push our teens toward experiences of self-giving any way we can. There is no alternative to the experience of giving to others—but the challenge is that teens will often not seek out such experiences on their own. To be sure, some will, and in those cases a parent's task will be different: helping the teen discern how to direct a desire to be of service to others, perhaps by sharing a passion for a cause. Other parents, though, will need to create opportunities and find ways to insist that their teens participate.

One of the images that Jesus uses in the gospels to illustrate what is worth loving involves a parent and a child. If a child asks for a fish, he says, no good parent will give the child a snake (Lk 11:11). Similarly, he says, we should ask God for what we desire. "And I tell you, ask and you will receive; seek and you will find; knock and the door will be opened to you" (Lk 11:9). Luke's version of this directive comes after Jesus teaches his disciples the Lord's Prayer, while the other evangelists include it in the context of longer exhortations about discipleship. The point seems to be: when our lives are centered on living as God has created us to live, our desires are expressions of the right longing for the purpose God has created us for. Our desires point us in the direction of blessing.

Teens are still in the process of developing self-knowledge, and so some expressions of desire may miss the mark, and reflect more a longing to be like their peers. But as attentive parents, we come to understand when they express more deeply rooted desires. In our case, an example was observing how Kris often liked to take pictures with his phone: he showed a very keen eye for detail, and his photos revealed to us beauty that we might have overlooked. Hoping to cultivate this gift, we were happy to say yes to him when he requested a camera for Christmas—and we have seen some wonderful pictures as a result. Of course it is too early to say whether he leverages this interest into a career or even an avocation, but for us it was important to encourage him to tell us what he desired, and to show him how to pursue those authentic desires in the direction of his growth as a person. We did that by simply taking delight in granting a desire that we could see gave him a way to explore his creativity, and perhaps learn some things along the way.

Responding to teens' expressions of desire will involve much more than giving presents. It will involve a willingness to enter into the fruits of their desires, good or bad. This is the essence of our discipleship as parents: walking intimately with our children through the challenges, struggles, and victories of their lives. Consider, for a moment, how you have already done this at various stages of your children's lives: celebrating birthdays, rejoicing at new friends, sorrowing at their injuries, waiting in expectant hope for news about a first day of school or joining a new team. Our emotional lives are caught up in theirs, and this is no different as they enter the teen years. Our own prayer lives will be enmeshed in their lives—so should our daily choices.

Please note: this doesn't mean that we are advocating for helicopter parenting, the destructive effects of which we have seen in college students. Don't hover and impose yourself. Don't intercede in their lives with the motivation of helping them avoid every possible mistake or misstep. That's a tragedy in kids' lives.

We are advocating for affective solidarity—that is, a posture of caring about our teens' lives enough to be strategic, creative, thoughtful, and judicious about how we walk with them in their pilgrimage toward adulthood. One important way we do this is by helping them to understand what is ultimately worth loving.

Pause and Consider

1. What are some of the things your teen wants? Can you sense what he or she really wants?

2. What do you see as emerging interests or talents? How might your support of these help your teen develop greater freedom and self-knowledge?

3. What are some things you hope your teen might try, in order to discover or develop talents? Are there ways you might find opportunities for that to happen without "helicoptering"?

Don't Be Afraid of Faith

Jesus' describes discipleship using a farming metaphor: a yoke which hitches two beasts of burden together. He describes the yoke as "light," unburdensome (Mt 11:30), particularly in contrast to a rigid approach to the law. One way of reading his description is by contrasting what he proposes to his disciples with the more prominent patterns of living among those who don't care much about holiness. "Hitching yourself to some ways of living," he seems to say, "is likely to be burdensome. But not my way."

We asked earlier whether we show our teens that it's good to be an adult and whether we model joy and freedom for them in our adult lives. Now, we raise a similar question: Do we show joy and freedom by choosing to root ourselves in the gospel? Recalling that talk is cheap, we rephrase it this way: Do our lives manifest a quiet confidence that our Catholic faith is the rock upon which we build our lives?

If this leaves you wanting specifics as to how one might do this, consider the following ways that you might offer your teens a model of faithful living:

- Do you take time to pray as a family, modeling a need to rely on God in good and bad times?

- Do you show your teens how your faith impels you to reach out to people in need, whether neighbors down the street or strangers at a soup kitchen?

- How do you celebrate religious holidays? Are they a source of celebration?

- Do your children see you spending time in quiet, private prayer?

- Are there religious symbols around your home, and do you share with your teens what they mean?

- Do you introduce topics of conversation related to faith or living faithfully?

- How do you practice forgiveness in your family? Do you go to Confession?

- Do you speak with generosity toward those who disagree with you? Do you show civility toward people of differing political opinions?

Notice that all of these are ways of behaving, actions we can take to be mindful of what we communicate. The actions we do lead to the persons we become—and they also become the foundation upon which our children build adult selves.

Living a faithful life does not mean living a perfect life. Our faith is centered on the Cross of Christ, a symbol of his rejection and execution. Rather than try to project a false perfection to our teens—a hopeless task, as they see through hypocrisy in an instant—our task is to show that a faithful life involves confronting all life's challenges with grace. In fact, we are doing our teens a service by entering into challenges with faith, holding faith even in the face of difficulty.

Throughout our professional lives, we have seen examples of young people encountering profound challenges, like the death of a loved one or a medical issue, which rock them to the core. At such times, the "architecture" of faith can provide comfort. By "architecture" we mean not so much specific things they may have learned in religious education classes but the core values that they imbibe from their families and their parents' dedication to a life of faith. They have learned: we should be loving; God is with us in times of stress; the Church is there to help us; the language of prayer might be the only language we can turn to during tragedy. These are very basic lessons learned not by the head, but by the heart.

One of the most common phrases Jesus uses throughout the gospels is some variation of "Don't be afraid." That is a message we ought to hear at every stage of life, but it's a particularly relevant message for teens, who are navigating significant challenges at the entrance to adulthood. How might we help them come to a faith that is at once rooted in the ancient traditions of the Church and still agile enough to help them live with freedom? How might you, we, as parents, anchor them in the faith that their lives are precious to God and that the gifts that they bring to the world are irreplaceable? How might we calm their fears that practicing faith will marginalize them among their peers? How might we show them that living Christ's faith opens us to the freedom to love others, to discern meaning in life, and to engage the most compelling questions fearlessly?

Peter's great proclamation of faith in Jesus was the question, "To whom shall we go? You have the words of eternal life" (Jn 6:68). Peter had come to see who Jesus was and what his message meant, and he had grown to believe that Jesus was the key to a life overflowing with meaning and love. It may take time for our teens to come to understand Peter's confession—or ours—but by providing the architecture of faith, we supply them with the framework within which they will continue to contemplate what is most meaningful in life. As they grow, our hope is that this architecture will provide the space within which they will continue to add meaningful experiences, relationships, and desires, so that they, too, might come to recognize that sharing their lives in friendship with God is indeed what makes our burdens light.

The Fruits of Faith

In Luke's gospel, Jesus uses a short parable about a fig tree to say something about how God looks for evidence of our repentance:

> There once was a person who had a fig tree planted in his orchard, and when he came in search of fruit on it but found none, he said to the gardener, "For three years now I have come in search of fruit on this fig tree but have found none. [So] cut it down. Why should it exhaust the soil?"
>
> He said to him in reply, "Sir, leave it for this year also, and I shall cultivate the ground around it and fertilize it; it may bear fruit in the future. If not you can cut it down." (Lk 13:6–9)

Jesus suggests with this image that our repentance and willingness to listen to God will bear fruit in our lives. It is a rather harsh image, with overtones of judgment and punishment of those who do not show any evidence.

We want to suggest a way of looking at this image for parents concerned that their teens' lives do not show evidence of faith. We know from contemporary studies that many teens and young adults are absent from church: their participation levels are the lowest among any age group. On some level, that is to be expected, given what we know about developmental psychology and faith formation.

Our interest is threefold. First, the parable may be described as emphasizing God's patience. The parable recalls Old Testament stories about bargaining with God, such as when Abraham talks down God from destroying Sodom (Gn 18:16–33). At face value, the owner of the orchard (God) is impatient while his gardener (who is like the prophets) is willing to do the work to keep him from exercising wrath. But if the parable follows the pattern of the Old Testament stories, then we can read the gardener's role as really being part of the master plan. Parents have the role of the gardener: we have the role of helping our teens bring forth fruit in their lives and are acting as agents of the master. Fortunately, we have more than a year to work with! It is helpful to consider that God is patient, working on our teens' hearts little by little.

Take Away

Elsewhere in the gospels, Jesus suggests that even a little faith—a "mustard seed," a small amount—can generate great fruit. Let us not ignore the mustard seeds in our teens' lives.

Second, we do well to consider our role as analogous to that of the gardener. Our teens are creations of God, sovereign creatures whom we can influence but ultimately not control. We can cultivate the ground, as suggested earlier in reference to the Parable of the Sower. We can use our energy and creativity to create conditions that might make them receptive to the Gospel—most prominently, by loving them always.

Third, *we cannot bring forth the fruit*. We may not even know what the fruit will be. What pains many parents and grandparents with whom we speak is that they consider the fruit to be regular participation in the liturgy of the Church, and they are grieved by the fact that their college- or post-college-aged children and grandchildren do not go to Mass. They often blame themselves. We suggest that it may take a long time for a person to really bring forth fruit, in the form of a generous life, a gentle spirit open to others, a great work that benefits people, or a lived vocation that draws others to Christ. There may be ways in which even those separated from the Church may bring forth fruit, ways which, over time, God will bless and use for the building of his kingdom.

This last point is particularly important for the ways that we hope our teens grow in freedom and responsibility and lead a happy life. The last thing we want to do is compromise their freedom; we do not want to get in the way of their growing into the people God has created them to be. Over time, parents come to understand the ways that children can challenge our limited means of understanding the world, and so on some level, we come to understand that their discernment process may nudge us to reconsider basic assumptions. We may have ideas about what they

need to do in school or in preparation for a career, perhaps
pointing them toward a major or a profession. We have
seen many examples over the years of teens getting into
conflicts with parents over the choice of a college major, for
example. Underneath these conflicts are usually basic ideas
about how to have a happy life, how to prioritize money
or relationships, or how to spend time or waste it. We've
had conversations with some of our students about what
they hope for—what fruit they wish to bring forth in their
lives—and are often amazed, even among those who may
have turned their backs on the Church at some point in
their teen years. We see evidence of enlarged hearts open
to helping others; tenacity and grit in overcoming difficult
challenges; hopefulness even after disappointment.

Perhaps the best example of teens who go on to bear
fruit as young adults even as they distance themselves
from the Church are several who have gone on to do
volunteer work. Sometimes what drives them out of the
Church is a sense that it is unjust, perhaps because of not
ordaining women or due to its understanding of sexuality. While we take a different view, we can nevertheless
appreciate the fact that they spend a year or more serving
in organizations like the Peace Corps or Jesuit Volunteer
Corps because they have accepted on a fundamental level
Jesus' call to serve the poor. Our hope is that living in this
mode of service will encourage them to develop a mature
faith that brings them back to the sacraments.

We must not give up on whatever fruit our teens will
eventually bring forth. We must pray for them always,
love them always, and continually till and fertilize the soil
around them in the hope of their bringing forth fruit. In

the end, we must place our hopes in God's hands, for he is the master of the garden.

What fruits of faith do you see, however immature? Do you see signs of

- self-giving?
- love toward friends or strangers?
- willingness to wear religious art (jewelry, body art)?
- a sense of service to the poor?
- perseverance in the face of difficulty?
- thankfulness for gifts of skill or character?
- other signs of your teen's character that make you proud?

Chapter Five

The Gift of the Body

Do you not know that your body is a temple of the holy Spirit within you, whom you have from God, and that you are not your own? For you have been purchased at a price. Therefore, glorify God in your body.

1 CORINTHIANS 6:19–20

Our teens make choices about their bodies during a period of rapid physical and emotional change. Tweens, especially, can be children in adult bodies, perceived by others in ways very different from how they perceive themselves. Also during these years, choices around sex, alcohol or drug use, fashion and body art, diet, exercise, and hygiene can have real consequences.

Toward Health and Holiness

In many ways, ours is a wonderful time for teens to come to awareness of the gift of the body. There are many role models—many more for young women, especially, compared to generations past. And with profound reflections coming, for example, from Pope John Paul II's Theology of the Body, there are many positive ways teens can develop an understanding of their bodies.

The constant prayer of Catholic parents is that our teens come to have a reverence for their bodies, treating them as gifts from God and not only as commodities to be manipulated. Here we will address some ways to consider our task as parents, rooting our own attitudes toward the body within an understanding that the entire physical world is a place suffused with grace, and therefore capable of being a place of encountering God. The logic is simple, but the task can be hard: all our choices about our bodies ought to reflect a profound sense of gratitude that God has graced us with this means of being present to one another. But because we live in a consumer-driven world, there are many who want us to treat our bodies not as gifts, but as products that can be used and changed at will to serve our unruly desires.

What we can expect is that we will constantly be working against the grain of popular culture. Our influence must be to promote an understanding of the natural beauty of the body and a smart critique of those who would suggest that our teens' bodies are inadequate, ugly, or to be used for fleeting pleasures. So we begin with a little theology, in order to sketch the picture of what God has revealed to us about what it means to be a person, body and soul.

The Body in Catholic Theology

At the heart of Christian theology is the person of Jesus, the God/man who, according to an early creedal formula "emptied himself, taking the form of a slave" (Phil 2:7) in order to lead a sinful humanity back into the arms of a loving Father. Throughout his ministry, Jesus reaches out to quite literally touch those in need of the Father's mercy: he smudges the eyes of a blind man with dirt and spittle and tells him to wash in the pool of Siloam to recover his sight (Jn 9:6–8); he touches lepers in order to heal them (Mt 8:2–3); he holds the hand of a girl who has died in order to raise her to life again (Mt 9:23–25); and he allows a woman with a hemorrhage to touch him in order to be healed (Mt 9:20–22). Again and again, Jesus manifests God's merciful love through touch, culminating with the gift of himself at the Last Supper, where he exhorts the disciples to take his very body and blood as a remembrance of the life he has lived. And in his death and resurrection—followed by stories such as his invitation to Thomas to see that he is still flesh and blood (Jn 20:24–29)—Jesus shows the theological importance of the body as the medium of divine grace.

The earliest forms of Christian teaching, symbolism, and art carry on the central importance of the body in Jesus' ministry. Much of the Church's theology of the first several centuries was concerned with understanding and proclaiming the story of who Jesus was in his incarnation, his taking on flesh. The doctrine of the Trinity—the understanding of God as Father, Son, and Holy Spirit—focused on the question of how the man Jesus, present in time and space through his humanness—could be the same God who created the cosmos and who was still present in human history through the gift of the Spirit.

Behind the many ecumenical councils that stretched from the early fourth century to the late eighth century were basic questions about how to understand Jesus' body and spirit and how to represent the story of Jesus through art so that people could come to know the Gospel. These councils unfolded amid other philosophical movements like Neoplatonism and various forms of Gnosticism that sought to deny the body and focus instead on a spiritual world as the locus of truth. What the early Church repeatedly stressed was the sacred truth of the physical world: not only of water, oil, bread, and wine—those physical elements which, through the sacraments, were bearers of divine grace—but also the human body itself.

For centuries, the Church wrestled with a thorny question: how could the body, with its lusts and distractions, nevertheless be the means by which the Lord of heaven and earth could enter into human history in order to lead us to salvation? Church leaders contemplated the story of the Nativity, marveling at the fact that God did not choose a magnificent chariot by which to enter into history but a humble young woman whose womb became a tabernacle. Jesus, through his mother Mary, experienced the glorious mess of childbirth. Under his parents' watchful eyes, he experienced diaper rash, potty training, and learning to speak, even while in exile from their home. He learned to walk and how to do rudimentary work with his father Joseph; he learned how to deal with cuts and bruises, how to run and play, and how to interact with friends. He navigated the usual peaks and valleys of puberty, became aware of the differences between boys and girls, and contemplated what his future would hold. He learned the Law of Moses, he became a *bar mitzvah*, and he began relating to others in Galilee as an adult.

In all this, Church leaders considered, Jesus was fully human, like us in all things but sin. For in Jesus' experience of humanness, he had no desire to sin. In his freedom, he fully embraced his humanness and found no room to desire anything that would compromise it. Did he experience sexual attractions? Probably, for there is no sin in that. Did he contemplate marriage? Most likely, since that was greatly prized in first-century Judaism. Was he privy to the kind of foul humor, innuendo, and chest-thumping that can sometime characterize male friendships? Probably, but undoubtedly he found ways to both engage with his friends and stay at arms' length from anything untoward. Jesus lived among us, in a world often beset by sin, always finding light and drawing others to it—so much so that he could later be described in John's gospel as "the light of the world" (Jn 8:12)—the one who was a perfect manifestation of God's light in a sometimes dark world.

Pause and Consider

1. How does contemplating Jesus' teen years impact the way you think about your teen? Does it make a difference to think about the challenging parts of parenting teens as somehow part of God's desire for the world, or for you?

2. Think back to your own teen years and the challenges you faced. In what ways are your teen's struggles similar?

3. What are the unique challenges your teen faces in this complex world? How do you think God desires to speak lovingly to him or her?

Our Teens' Growing Bodies

We have many visceral memories of our children's growing up years. Life with babies is an education in bodily
fluids; life with toddlers is an exercise in constant picking
up and moving our children; life with young kids involves
lots of running; life with older kids means lots of driving. There is a constant physicality to parenthood—don't
you think?—involving both positive (hugs, cuddling,
goodnight kisses) and negative (bad smells, loud noises,
thoughtless gestures). We know how parenting is a physically demanding vocation.

But there is also something profoundly sacramental
about parenting. The sacraments, remember, are celebrations throughout the Church's life that center on the ministry of Christ and that provide physical, tangible focal
points for grace: the water of Baptism, the oil of Confirmation, the bread and wine of Eucharist. Most remark-
ably, perhaps, is an even more basic observation that is
underneath any experience of parenting: the very life of
the family is predicated on sex, celebrated sacramentally
in marriage.

We do not mean to suggest that a sacramental marriage is the only context in which children are born, nor do
we mean that all sex is sacramental. As adoptive parents,
we know all too well that children can enter a family's life
in many different ways. But every child exists because
of sexual union—even when that union is made possible
through technology, and every child exists because of cells
that come from a mother and a father. We marvel at this
mystery at the root of all human life and marvel at the
ways that our bodies carry the capacity to participate in
the mystery of creation. Our own bodies—and the bodies

of our children—carry this mystery and so are worthy of reverence.

During the teen years, the rapid change we see our children's bodies undergoing is no less marvelous. Sometimes, after being away on a trip, we have come home amazed at the fact that it seems that our children have become a little bit more adult-looking, and we let them know it. We want to share with them not only how much we delight in them, but also how much we reverence the mystery that they are. That mystery is both a source of wonder and sadness—and our children are aware of both. They understand that their growing bodies are making them more capable of things: being stronger or faster or more attractive. But they are also aware that with their growth comes loss of childhood. Our most obvious example is that all of them like to be carried to bed, even as they recognize that it is becoming more and more difficult for Dad to do it. They recognize a greater freedom to do more "teen-like" things, such as going to the beach with friends, but also feel a loss when they recognize that they are far more self-conscious about being in bathing suits than they were in their carefree youth.

Very early in our parenting, we began sharing that basic message by using the phrase "Use your powers for good." It was a broad, positive message, meant to suggest that they have powers to influence others—by being friendly or mean, by sharing or hoarding toys, and so on. On a subtle level, we were also trying to convey the idea that the powers they have are gifts to be shared. Speaking sweetly, showing a puppy-dog face, complimenting others—all these things kids learn can be used to manipulate others. "Use your powers for good," we would remind them, is a way of showing reverence for ourselves and for others, and by being ready to discover the presence of God in those around us.

Even now, as they navigate a world of maturing relationships, we will sometimes haul out that old phrase as a reminder that while the situation has changed, the basic moral posture has not. They are still to recognize that they have powers that can influence others but that they have the responsibility to reverence themselves and those around them. Today, the powers may include the ability to draw attention from others by the way they dress or act; the ability to make others feel important or worthless in group chats; the ability to include or exclude at school; and so on. Our message is still the same.

For Reflection and Conversation

1. What did your teen look like a year or two ago? What has changed, both in the way he or she looks and in the kind of person he or she is?

2. Do you see signs of your teen feeling nostalgic for when he or she was younger? Do you see signs of fear of getting older? What might you do to help your teen navigate that transition?

Dealing with Body Anxieties

> The lamp of the body is the eye. If your eye is sound, your whole body will be filled with light; but if your eye is bad, your whole body will be in darkness. And if the light in you is darkness, how great will the darkness be. . . . Therefore I tell you, do not worry about your life, what you will eat [or drink], or about your body, what you will wear. Is not life more than food and the body more than clothing? (Mt 6:22–25)

It is not easy being a teen in a world that induces anxiety about the body. We see this anxiety on a regular basis, both in our students and in our own kids, from concerns about clothing, exercise, makeup, perfume, hairstyle, manicures and pedicures, and so on. Our task as parents is to offer constant reminders to reverence their bodies and to come to understand them as a central part of their giftedness as human beings.

How tragic it is when young people do not see themselves in their full beauty! We have been struck by the fragility of teens' sense of themselves, constantly measuring themselves against unrealistic expectations of what constitutes beauty. Sometimes it is physical beauty they seek, seduced as they are by the photoshopped, airbrushed fictions that abound in the digital world. One source projects the beauty market at 265 billion dollars in 2017[1]—and that's just for personal care products, not including services like plastic surgery, beauty salons, or the fitness industry, which together represent another 70 billion dollars each year in the United States alone. In a period of life when everyone has a natural tendency to question themselves, is it any wonder that so many teens are influenced by the obsession with looks?

As parents, we must push back against this tendency reminding our teens that their beauty comes from being created by a loving God and called into relationship. Their self-worth comes not from their looks, their SAT scores, their athletic abilities, or their talents—any of the usual ways through which they glance nervously around them and measure themselves. Their worth comes from the simple fact of being alive, capable of being loved by God.

Nowhere will they discern their lovableness more than in the ways that their parents interact with them on a daily basis. Our love will be healing for them if it is manifested in concrete, constant, even (as we described earlier) transgressive ways. We must be like the Father in the story of the Prodigal Son: excessive, foolish, over-the-top. To heal our teens' tendency toward insecurity—magnified every day on TV and billboards as well as in movies, video games, and magazines—we must remind them how beautiful they are. Who else in their lives is likely to do this?

When Jesus describes the eye as the "lamp of the body" he means this in both a literal and metaphorical sense. It is through the eye that a person takes in an understanding of the world. But the eye is not simply a camera lens: the way we see depends on the manner in which we seek to understand. We must teach our children to see as we do, starting early in their lives and continuing through their teen years.

A recent example comes to mind: Kris was making the observation that a new kid at school was having a hard time getting around. We pressed a bit, wondering what she saw. Did she see someone who needed a friend, a helping hand, a compassionate voice? (That was certainly our hope.) Or did she see someone who was just out of it, likely to be the object of laughter or mean jokes? We were happy to learn that she tried to reach out to the new kid with a friendly word.[2]

This small example leads to larger questions. What are the experiences that shape the way our teens view the world? What do they see around them? Whom do they imitate? What are the models they pursue? What are the rewards they seek? Whose approval do they desire? What do they consider beautiful?

Anne Becker, a researcher at Harvard Medical School, has done two studies of teen girls in Fiji, looking at how media consumption affects their body image. She chose Fiji because television had only been introduced there in 1995, and so she could study how first-generation exposure to American TV impacted girls. What she learned was disturbing: in this otherwise traditional society in which there was a large preoccupation with food, girls exposed to shows like *Beverly Hills 90210* and *Melrose Place* (remember those?) began experiencing dysmorphia—unhealthy attitudes toward their bodies. What's more, her research found that the impact was not limited to those who actually watched TV—it also impacted friend groups. The introduction of American TV elicited unhealthy desires to emulate the characters, even among girls who had never even watched the shows.[3]

What Becker suggests is how potentially destructive media consumption can be. We must be careful, though. Our challenge as parents is not to leap to broad conclusions but to enter our teens' lives with discerning eyes. It is too easy to conclude that all forms of media are bad and try to keep them from our children's eyes. We know parents who do not have TV in their homes, for example. This may be a good choice—it's one we ourselves have made at times. But with media saturation in our society, it is also true that our teens will have access to all sorts of media throughout their days, either at school or at friends' homes or at various public places. From our perspective, the more important posture is to "vaccinate" them—offering small doses of media consumption—in order to help them learn the experience of different forms of media use. We want to help them understand the ways that various media figures—producers of TV shows, hosts of Internet sites, makers of video games, entertainers, actors—try to shape their imagination. In doing so, we hope to make them aware of the ways that many of these figures are trying to make them anxious about their bodies so they will buy things.

We agree with Sr. Hosea M. Rupprecht that it can be instructive to watch movies or shows with kids.[4] Not long ago, we finished watching the sitcom *Friends* with our teens. We were surprised to learn that one of them had begun streaming the series, and immediately, we began anxiously remembering episodes that had themes we felt were beyond what someone of that age should be watching. But instead of forbidding Kris from watching it (a move which might have instead led her to watch it secretly), we decided to all watch together.

It was a good experience. Remembering the series we had watched when we were younger was an education in how age changes your perspective. Watching it again with teens elicited from us a great deal more discomfort than we had ever experienced as twentysomethings. We would sometimes make a comment on something we saw: "Where on earth is Rachel hiding her baby all this time she's hanging out with her friends?" We lent an adult perspective to their understanding of the drama. What we took away from the experiment was a larger point about how our role as parents is fundamentally about entering into our teens' lives. We were saying, in effect, *you are important to us, and we want to walk with you toward adulthood.* We wanted to answer the anxiety-inducing voices that abound in various media, to say something like, *You are perfect the way you are. Do not be anxious about looking like Monica or Rachel.*

To use a different example, when watching a major sporting event (which is much more likely to elicit reactions from our son), we wanted to communicate: *You need not be a great athlete to be valuable. You are a gift from God as you are.* In both instances, the point was that we wanted to be the voice that assuages the anxiety that teens may feel when they try to measure themselves against the role models—good or bad—that are instantly and perpetually accessible, literally in the palms of their hands through their devices. We want them to be able to distance themselves from that anxiety and rest secure in the constant refrain, *We love you for who you are now and for who you will be as you grow.*

For Reflection and Conversation

1. What are the experiences that shape the way your teens view the world? What do they see around them? Whom do they imitate? What are the models they pursue? What are the rewards they seek? Whose approval do they desire? What do they consider beautiful?

2. What media influence your teen? What artists, movies, shows, websites, or social media platforms are go-to sources?

3. What are some opportunities you might create to share an experience of technology (movie, show, game, etc.) with your teen, helping him or her to experience that medium through your eyes?

You Are the Body of Christ

> As a body is one though it has many parts, and all the
> parts of the body, though many, are one body, so also
> Christ. . . . If they were all one part, where would the
> body be? But as it is, there are many parts, yet one
> body. The eye cannot say to the hand, "I do not need
> you," nor again the head to the feet, "I do not need
> you." Indeed, the parts of the body that seem to be
> weaker are all the more necessary, and those parts of
> the body that we consider less honorable we surround
> with greater honor, and our less presentable parts are
> treated with greater propriety, whereas our more pre-
> sentable parts do not need this. But God has so con-
> structed the body as to give greater honor to a part that
> is without it, so that there may be no division in the
> body, but that the parts may have the same concern
> for one another. If [one] part suffers, all the parts suffer
> with it; if one part is honored, all the parts share its joy.
> Now you are Christ's body, and individually parts of
> it. (1 Cor 12:12, 19–27)

There are a number of recent studies to suggest that adult
Americans are becoming lonelier.[5] For teens, while they
have many connections, they have fewer friends than in
earlier generations.[6] What we observe in studies like these
has to do with changes in the ways people relate to one
another as a consequence of technology. What this suggests for teens is that they may well feel very connected
and therefore less lonely than their parents or grandparents at the same age—but that sense of connectedness may
mask a lack of real relationship, and it may contribute to
the feeling of isolation that one college student reported
when describing what it's like when her phone runs out
of power. Whereas once the feeling of loneliness might

have been an inducement to seek out friendship, today it is an experience of dread resulting from addiction to technological means.

In the text from his first letter to the Corinthian church, just above, Saint Paul uses a strong image for the nascent Christian community: they are Christ's living body, even after his Resurrection and Ascension. What he means is that every person has a vital role to play within that body, much like the different cells or organs within a human body. He's making a theological and anthropological point: namely, that God has created each person to be a vital, living part that contributes to the good of the whole. No person is accidental; no member of the Church is marginal. All contribute to the body.

This is a striking image in a virtual age and one that is suggestive for parents of teens. Do your teens have a strong sense that their lives are critical for the kind of work that God wants to do in the world? That they have a mission that they alone can undertake just by being themselves?

We are struck by how much of our teens' lives and friendships are spent on devices, even when we set limits on their use. As a rule, we tend to prefer physical activity to virtual activity, but our learning curve—since people of our generation are "digital immigrants" compared to our kids who are "digital natives"—has been to recognize that not all virtual interactions are the same. Initially, we wrestled with whether we wanted them to have iPhones, for example, but quickly came to realize that lacking a phone meant, effectively, lacking access to group chats by which the majority of social life among teens is planned. No technology, no social capital.

What we've grudgingly come to realize is that their devices do, in fact, help them negotiate the skills and practices of relationship forming and building. While there is a part of us that wishes that they could go out the door and interact with real people, we realize that one great benefit of technology is the fact that it enables them to keep in touch with classmates and friends across town and across the world. There is an attractiveness to being virtually connected. At the same time, though, we have concerns about the extent to which we see our teens interacting with others through devices. To use one example: One of our teens has made some great friends and is constantly interacting with them on group chats. But what we see when they are together is that they seem unable to extricate themselves from their devices—they interact with each other, yes, but with another eye on their phones to interact with others in their group who are not physically present. That inability to simply be in the present moment with the people around them strikes us as a concern.

So we see both benefits and liabilities to technology. Rather than get rid of it entirely, our strategy has shifted to a kind of rationing system, which means that our teens may not be on any device past a certain hour in the evening, or before a certain hour in the morning. And we have always emphasized that we monitor all their activity. We set parental controls to block pornography and other malicious activity; we check their phones regularly; we educate ourselves about hidden apps, in-game purchases, and so on. We have found it important to stay abreast of teen online practices, learning from various school programs and blogs about adolescent media consumption. We consider all these steps part of being with them on their journey through the teen years.

In the bigger picture, what we hope to convey is that virtual media are fundamentally different from flesh-and-blood persons. More than once we've interrupted Kris to say, "Use the actual phone part of the phone!"—for while a phone is still not a person, it is at least one step closer to human interaction than texting. We are trying to send a message that a technological medium is still a *medium*, a go-between, something that stands in the middle of two people communicating. We want them to understand that even bodies are media between two persons—even bodies "stand in the middle" and may either help or hurt a relationship.

The key message we are sending is that through their bodies they establish communion with others. Much of the experimentation we see teens doing in American culture—from drugs or alcohol to use of technology, sex, body art, and various forms of self-harm or dysmorphia—we see as rooted in unformed self-understanding. For when a person comes to truly understand the body as the manifestation of our personhood in space and time—that is, the way we present our selves to the world—it is impossible not to reverence the body. For the Christian, the body is the very locus of the incarnation, the very means by which the Lord of heaven and earth came to share intimately with us, breaking bread and experiencing death. Our bodies are thus a share in the incarnated life and the means by which we enter into communion with one another. Our bodies are places for contemplative wonder, rather than manipulative control.

It is probably impossible to imagine easy ways to communicate this message, so for us it has meant consistent, reinforcing, deepening forms of communication with our teens. Infrequently it has meant lecturing, though when we see problems we will have a serious talk. More often, it's meant making observations or raising questions.

For example, at various times our teens have talked about piercings or tattoos. Our answer has been to talk about how these are permanent choices for what may be temporary desires. To use another example, when conversations about playing sports have come up, we've talked about how our love for sports must not overshadow other concerns like schoolwork, family time, or finances.

In all, we are trying to help them become discerning in their attitude toward their own and other people's bodies, mindful that people are inherently valuable flesh-and-blood creatures who need one another and desire good relationships. That fundamental ethic begins with the way they regard themselves, and includes the consistent message that their bodies are the primary means by which they enter into relationship with others—speaking rather than texting, making eye contact, and so on. It means honoring their bodies with diet and exercise, being thoughtful about the use of makeup, and being aware of how their clothing choices are forms of communication. It means that sports, while fun and even formative, are but one element in their lives and in our family's life. It means that sex is a privileged, sacramental form of encounter between husband and wife, as well as a prophetic sign for the Church and the world: a pearl of great price, very much worth preparing oneself for in the teen years.

For Reflection and Conversation

1. What do you observe about the ways your teen engages in relationships with others, of the same age or of different ages?

2. Do you have concerns about your teen's screen use? Is it masking an unwillingness to truly engage with people in real time?

Talking about Sex

Our strategy since our children were young has been to communicate a positive, hope-filled message about sex. We have no illusions about the increasingly corrosive messages abroad in popular culture: messages that, even today, astonish us as to what has become the new normal. But rather than using language likely to strike our teens as prudish, we've decided to go on the offensive. Our job is to help them come to appreciate sex as the gift that it is: a gift of God by which husbands and wives participate in creation and by which they draw closer into a union which, in both the Old and New Testaments, is the closest analogy to describe God's longing for intimate communion with human persons.

Sex impacts not only those who engage in it, but also the family and community as a whole. Our message stresses that it is never something that individuals choose exclusively for themselves; it impacts the ways that they engage with others—including (and especially) the children who may be conceived.

How do we strike a balance between promoting an attitude of sexual responsibility, on the one hand, and a hopeful attitude that sees the body as a gift and a source of delight within a marriage—a pearl of great price worth ordering one's life toward, even at an early age? We do this, primarily, through practices that manifest how this understanding has shaped our own marriage. We have always been physically affectionate, both toward each other and toward our children. And while the ways we show affection toward our teens has evolved, what has not changed is our regular use of touch to demonstrate how much we love them: hugs and kisses good night, hair brushing, back rubs, and so on. The way we as a couple hold hands or share other visible forms of affection reinforces the idea that we find our physical relationship a source of joy. But we have also taken specific opportunities to reinforce our message with conversations about sex— from the earliest "talk" with our pre-adolescents to more complex explorations of why we have made the sexual choices we have in light of the Church's understanding of sexuality. Sex has never been a forbidden topic in our home; we address it whenever we have the opportunity, especially now that our teens are past the age of raising questions about it unselfconsciously.

The fact that so many teenage experiences of desire are imitative means that friend groups and social media influences will have an impact on their experience of sexual desire. Where we see this influence in a particularly corrosive way is in the impact of pornography, especially on young men. We are still at an early stage of research on the extent of this influence, but what is clear is that the many ministries seeking to heal people of porn addiction is a sign of how powerful that tendency can become.[7] Not everyone falls into addictive patterns, but what this phenomenon points to are the ways that desire can be shaped by perception.

We've had conversations with Kris about the sexual practices of peers and the experience of feeling out-of-touch with the crowd. That feeling will be unavoidable in a community under the influence of peer pressure—and so our task becomes helping Kris come to a reinforced understanding of the great goods to be gained by maintaining a robust and hopeful attitude toward sex. Our message is never simply "No!" or "Just wait till you're married!" Our message is "Grow wonderful relationships." We are convinced that authentic friendships, and eventually romantic relationships, provide the emotional, psychological, and spiritual benefits that feed our souls in ways that uncommitted sexual encounters cannot.[8] Our hope and prayer for our teens is that they will give energy to being and having authentic relationships, so that their sexual choices will naturally fall into rhythm with what the Church has handed on since the time of Jesus.

What we see among teens is experimentation, which, as has happened in previous ages, reflects a natural curiosity and desire to explore what various experiences of desire might mean. But the problem today is that such experimentation often happens in contexts that can preserve a young person's errors forever. An errant Snapchat that gets copied and shared, a supposedly private message that a friend or parent accidentally sees, a Tweet or Instagram photo that goes way beyond the bounds of what the person intended—all are examples of how the price of experimentation has become dangerous. Teens often lack the wisdom to understand what's really private; but more importantly, they lack an understanding of the symbolism of the body.

Recently, we were on a trip to see a waterfall and had a great time splashing around. Our teens were taking lots of pictures that they intended to share with their friends. We were pleased when one of them came up and showed us a picture that she intended to post on Instagram, asking, effectively, "Is this one appropriate?" We had talked about how posting pictures in bathing suits was inviting trouble—that between some judging how good you look and others making inappropriate comments, it was a good idea to avoid it altogether. We were reminded of an exchange earlier in the week when some friends of hers had, in fact, made some comments online that hurt one of her other friends. We asked whether she had any part in the incident and talked about how it might be a good idea to reach out to the friend and ensure that the offhanded comments didn't injure their relationship. The point we were trying to raise was that virtual interactions have real-life consequences for flesh-and-blood people.

In anthropological language, the body is the symbol of the person and the text or picture is a representation of the symbol. Think about the frighteningly common phenomenon of sexting—sending a provocative picture via text message. The picture is twice removed from the person: it's a photo of a person's body, and the body is the way the person is visible to others. As teens are learning the language of the body's symbolism, from the way a person dresses to the way he or she uses facial expressions and the like, they are coming to understand more and more how persons use their bodies to communicate with others. There is a natural complexity to learning the language of

the body. Now add to that complexity a further compli-
cation: the fact that a person has taken a picture of a body
and sent it via social media. Is it saying:

"I look good"?

Or "I like you"?

Or "I am comfortable enough in my own skin to share
it with others"?

Or "I want to have sex with you"?

Or something else?

Now add to that complexity the psychological, developmental reality of the teen years. Is whatever the teen is
trying to communicate reflective of a thoughtful, reflective
judgment about his or her well-being? Is it representative
of a mature understanding of relationships or the connection between sexual desire and the desire for love? Does it
take into account what they are likely to deem important
many years from now, or does it reflect hormone-induced
impulse?

Our constant prayer is that our regular willingness
to talk about sex will help our teens develop a discerning
attitude, one that minimally suggests caution when experiencing curiosity. No topic is ever off the table—we have
approached all the themes we've addressed above, as well
as teen pregnancy, abortion, birth control, homosexuality,
and transgender issues. In all, we hope to connote a position that balances truth and pastoral sensitivity. Never will
we accuse anyone baldly of sinning, but we will use the
language of the Church's understanding of what God has
revealed about the body and relationships.

In recent months, we've had some opportunities to
broach the subject with Kris, after he made the observation that many of his friends were already sexually active.

We found the tenor of the conversation positive: Kris was reflecting on the fact that he felt a disjunction with where his friends were. Without our saying anything, he recognized that his friends' choices were not conducive to their greatest well-being, nor that of the people with whom they were sexually active. Neither we nor he spoke about sin or Catholic morality specifically; we were able simply to talk about what good relationships look like in the broad context of a life oriented toward happiness and, one day, toward being part of a family of one's own discerning.

Toward Health and Holiness

The way that Jesus dealt with sexual morality is evidenced in the story of the woman caught in adultery. "Let the one among you who is without sin be the first to throw a stone at her," he said—but he also held that the law given by Moses was to obeyed. He did not judge, but he did observe what God ordained about sex being ordered toward marriage as it was in the beginning (see Jn 8:1–11 and Mt 19:7–9).

Like Jesus in the stories of the Samaritan woman and the woman caught in adultery, we hope that conversations about truth are also invitations to a deepening of relationship with a God who loves us enough to show us how to use our bodies for the sake of building relationships and communities.

For Reflection and Conversation

1. What conversations have you had with your teen about sex?

2. What conversations do you still need to have?

3. How might you model a good approach to sexuality in your life and in your home?

Chapter Six

When Life Is Hard

The Gospel—the "Good News" (*euangelion* in the Greek of the New Testament)—is fundamentally a story of God entering into the story of human history and inviting people into friendship with him. The back story, of course, is about how people decide they know better than God what a happy life is like and go their own way quite in spite of how much God stamps his feet and yells at them to clean up their act.

Ignatian Insight

The goal of Ignatian spirituality is friendship with God and a willingness to go where the Lord sends us in order to participate in building the world God desires. Rather than avoiding the messes of the world, God calls us to enter into them and transform them through love. Parenting well is one way to respond to God's call.

If that story sounds familiar, you're not alone. The entire story of the Old Testament sounds a lot like the relationship between parents and adolescents. God creates people and a loving home for them. God gives them rules and points out what will cause them harm. God says, "Don't do this one thing," and so of course they do it. God gets angry and sends them away, but not before equipping them with the means to make a life for themselves. Over time, God finds ways to reach out to them and draw them back into relationship, but again and again the people find ways to disregard what he says.

Yet God is relentless in pursuing them: over and over, he reaches out and does his best to speak to them. Again and again, the people do whatever they feel like doing because they are free. God erupts in anger, even to the point of nearly destroying the world, but he later regrets his actions and tries a different approach. Figures like Jacob and Jeremiah complain that they just don't understand God; figures like Solomon and David are basically good people who make terrible mistakes; figures like Ruth and Esther show nobility of character; characters like Job and Susanna are good people who experience injustice and suffering. In short, the Old Testament is the long story of a relationship between a loving parent who is often frustrated by the way his children behave but who still wants to see them grow and prosper. The characters of this long story are all of us at some time in our lives.

So, you see, we all know what it is like to be a teen at some very deep level!

As parents of teens, now, we also live within this long, familiar story. At times, we will recall moments from our own teen years when we see ourselves suddenly occupying the dreaded role our own parents once held. ("Am I really telling my kid to turn the music down?") Maybe we see them making mistakes similar to ones we made at that age. Maybe we experience the fear that might have eluded us at fifteen or seventeen or nineteen—fear that arises from the greater understanding that comes with age.

We sometimes find ourselves in a position similar to the God of the Old Testament: the loving parent whose children disregard his rules, who longs to find a way to get through to them. He has created them and given them freedom, but now they use their freedom to go their own way and leave the parent behind.

Several of Jesus' parables speak to the situation God finds himself in—and which we often find ourselves in as well. Probably the most well-known is the Parable of the Prodigal Son, about the adolescent who demands his inheritance and then runs off and squanders it (Lk 15:11–32). It's a parable about the prodigality of the father—that is, the excessive generosity of the father—whose response of throwing a party for the son when he returns is not likely to reflect recommendations of developmental psychologists on how to discipline wayward adult children. What the parable highlights, though, is something that we do well to remember when life with our teens is hard: namely, that in spite of all difficulties, the fundamental vocation of the parent is to rejoice at the very being of our children. Before any consideration of what they do, we must celebrate the very fact of their existence—to say, in essence, "It is so good that you are here." In a world that judges people by what they accomplish, this fundamental role of the parent is a sanctuary of holiness, one through which we, too, will become holy.

Another image that Jesus uses of God's predicament is the Parable of the Ungrateful Tenants.

[A] man planted a vineyard, leased it to tenant farmers,
and then went on a journey for a long time. At harvest
time he sent a servant to the tenant farmers to receive
some of the produce of the vineyard. But they beat
the servant and sent him away empty-handed. So he
proceeded to send another servant, but him also they
beat and insulted and sent away empty-handed. Then
he proceeded to send a third, but this one too they
wounded and threw out. The owner of the vineyard
said, "What shall I do? I shall send my beloved son;
maybe they will respect him." But when the tenant
farmers saw him they said to one another, "This is the
heir. Let us kill him that the inheritance may become
ours." So they threw him out of the vineyard and killed
him. (Lk 20:9–15)

The parable is ostensibly about the history of Israel and
their consistent tendency to disregard and mistreat the
servants of God.

Have you ever felt like the owner of the vineyard,
astonished at your ungrateful teen children? Have you had
the experience of wondering how your years of care and
attention to your teen are repaid by a bad decision? Have
you expressed frustration at how little your teen seems to
get what you are teaching about life, making decisions that
fly in the face of what you believe?

What we know from developmental psychology is
that on some level, the job description of the teen is to come
to a stronger sense of self in part through distancing from
parents. Growth in freedom comes only as a result of such
distancing. But while most parents understand the importance of teens developing a sense of identity separate from
parents, still there are limits that we all have in our minds.
We've had conversations with many parents over the years

about teens not just pushing limits but obliterating them through bad choices. In recent memory, we can think of families who are dealing with eating disorders, cutting, suicide attempts, drug use, driving under the influence of alcohol, theft, sexual acting out, and many other difficult situations.

It is a testament to the power of the parenting vocation that parents who face such problems do not simply write off their teens as lost causes. Facing a teen's poor choices can elicit a kind of steely resolve and a willingness to double down as a loving parent. In our own case, facing situations that make life hard are summons to return powerfully to prayer, to turn the situation over to God, and to make hard choices about how to run toward our teen like the prodigal father, with an irresponsible love. This final chapter is about finding resources for that love through deepening our understanding of the challenges teens face—and deepening our dependence on a God who knows intimately what it means to love someone who does not always love back.

Whom Can Teens Trust?

> Beware of false prophets, who come to you in sheep's clothing, but underneath are ravenous wolves. By their fruits you will know them. Do people pick grapes from thornbushes, or figs from thistles? Just so, every good tree bears good fruit, and a rotten tree bears bad fruit. A good tree cannot bear bad fruit, nor can a rotten tree bear good fruit. Every tree that does not bear good fruit will be cut down and thrown into the fire. So by their fruits you will know them. (Mt 7:15–20)

Twenty-three centuries ago, Aristotle made prescient observations about young people that are as true today as they were then. Speaking of the ways in which young people enter into friendships, he recognized that they are guided by emotion and look for pleasure. They pursue whatever they find most interesting—but that may quickly change, and thus so do their friendships. They fall in and out of love, even within the course of a day, but still want more than anything to have friends.[1]

We've seen the wisdom of the philosopher's observations both at home and in our professional lives. On one level, what he describes is perfectly natural: teens are learning the ways their emotions work and can have wild mood swings within the span of a few minutes. We've certainly observed Kris laughing and chatty one minute and breathing fire the next. We've seen group chats where there is good humor and silliness, frequently involving acronyms and emojis—and then drama about who excluded whom, ANGRY TEXTS IN ALL CAPS!!!!, and threats about someone being excluded from the friendship group the next day.

Young teens are particularly susceptible to following wherever their emotions lead them. We have seen many times the way Kris's emotions can erupt in any direction: anger at a friend becomes anger at whoever happens to be in the room at that moment. Anxiety about a test becomes general anxiety directed toward everyone. Are we really that much different? We sometimes have to simply say something like, "Act how you must; don't act how you feel." Part of the point is just that teens need to be able to practice the skills appropriate for social behavior regardless of whatever is the predominating emotion.

The great difficulty we face, though, has to do with the fact that teens are surrounded by things that prey on their as-yet untamed emotions. For boys, there are the constant toxic messages surrounding sports culture, most evident in ads during major sporting events. Beer, body spray, video games, cars, sports-betting websites—these and many other commodities are hawked with slick ads that attract boys' attention to cool lifestyles, gorgeous women, and promises of bling. For girls, the drive toward beauty manifests itself in a host of problems in the college years, from eating disorders to muscle dysmorphia (a compulsion toward excessive exercise), to various forms of anxiety. The portrayal of models in magazines and websites, the chronic underrepresentation of intelligent women in film and TV,[2] gender bias in sports, and many other factors impact the way teen girls are able to imagine themselves as adults. There are many wolves in sheep's clothing, tempting teens with promises of wealth or beauty or sexual power—and as parents, we have to help them to pay attention to the real fruit they offer.

This is no small task. In fact, from our experience, it's a relentless one. We wrote earlier about watching TV with our teens as one strategy for bringing a critical voice to their imaginations, our hope being that we might help "name the wolves" whose interest is their money rather than their well-being. The difficulty is that naming the wolves is like hitting a moving target; our teens grow so fast that they gain and lose interest in things quickly. Most elusive, we find, are musical tastes. It is almost impossible to learn every song on their playlists and inquire what sort of depravity is being peddled.

It's impossible to always play defense. While we believe there are precautions that parents can take—like using parental controls on devices and computers, having regular conversations about what teens are doing with friends, or tying free time to work around the house—the more important strategy is the long-term one of cultivating teens' imaginations of what is most meaningful in life. That means praying for them always, both on your own and in visible ways that help them understand how much you love them. For us, it means not letting a day go by without blessing them, usually at bedtime, with a simple prayer, "Lord, bless Kris," making the Sign of the Cross on the forehead.

It also means trying relentlessly to bring people into Kris's life who can help her see a world beyond the one most immediate to her at school or on TV. Coaches, camp counselors, friends and friends' parents, people at church—these are our resources. On one occasion, Kris had to do a school assignment that involved interviewing a veteran, and it provided an opportunity to converse with a relative whom she'd known simply at family gatherings. That conversation opened an entirely new way of seeing the relative, and the chance to talk about something serious like going off to war and dealing with dangerous situations was eye opening.

One learning curve for us has been leveraging school projects as opportunities to have conversations about big topics. Not long ago, we took advantage of a unit on the Holocaust to have important conversations about the nature of sin and evil and the need to form our consciences in order to not fall into patterns of dangerous groupthink.

We sat around the kitchen table one evening and explored the issues of that historical event together. We asked questions of Kris, and we were able to engage around them in a variety of ways. What follows is a snapshot of what we remember from that conversation. While not verbatim, it tries to capture the way we use an opportunity to talk about important things.

> Kris: "I just can't believe this actually happened. Look at these pictures!"
>
> Mom and Dad: "I know. It's hard to see them. Sometimes, it seems, people allow themselves to do what's evil. It's one reason why we think it's so important to talk about sin, because it can lead to horrible evil."
>
> Kris: "Why would God let this happen?"
>
> Mom and Dad: "We can't know that. But we can see that it happens not because of something God does but because of the choices human beings make. And so we want to train ourselves always to make loving choices informed by a good understanding of what real people face in their lives. It's one of the important reasons we go to Mass every week—to train ourselves to see the world the way Jesus did. Why do you think this happened?"
>
> Kris: "We're learning about Adolf Hitler and the Nazis and how they hated Jews. They thought they could solve their country's problems by killing off people they hated."
>
> Mom and Dad: "What does that suggest to you about hate?"
>
> Kris: "That it makes a lot more sense when Jesus talks about loving your enemies."

We intend to do this sort of thing much more often now that we know how well it can work!

Other times, a news story generates a conversation about difficult topics like terrorism, drug use, or driving safety. Sometimes we just have to dive into chances as they arise, in order to talk about moral choices.

While we try to be diligent about helping our teens understand wolves in sheep's clothing, the plain fact is that we are often worried about them. We can't pretend that we've got it all figured out; in fact, quite the opposite—which is why we have found that parenting calls for regular prayer. We can't protect our kids from everything—and even if we could, it wouldn't be good for them. We can try to prepare them to face evil but also recognize that God is laboring to deal directly with them and draw them into intimate relationship.

Prayer and Parenting

The prayer that is appropriate for parents is conversation with God about daily life with its usual challenges and opportunities. That is why the examen can be so helpful for parents: it helps us see our daily lives with graced understanding.

Parenting teens is a peculiar way to identify with the prominent biblical image of God as a parent. We desperately want their good, and there is a part of us that would eagerly choose to preserve them from any harm. But we also recognize the need for them to develop their freedom in order to grow fully and enter into mature relationships. So, too, with God, who throughout the Old Testament sees their freedom abused and who nevertheless finds a way to save them and draw them back into a covenantal relationship. God never, never gives up on Israel, even though there are times when he seems quite ready to do so. In the end, he is willing to die for them in order to bring them back home to him. That story, at the heart of Christian faith, is the source of hope that we parents have even when the stories of our teens' lives may appear dark. God finds a way.

Pause and Consider

1. What or who are some of the influences on your teen's life that you find most troubling?

2. What are some specific ways you can pray for your teen to resist those influences?

Seeing the Wheat among the Weeds

In the Our Father, a key line is our petition that God "forgive us our trespasses as we forgive those who trespass against us." Throughout the gospels, Jesus talks about the mercy of the Father, who is willing to erase our sins and restore us to friendship with no questions asked. That posture of mercy is what we pray for every time we pray the Our Father, and it points to a challenge and an opportunity in daily interactions with our teens. Will they make bad choices? Yes. But will we continue to love them and be willing to start each day anew? Yes—because that is exactly how God deals with us. Jesus' Parable of the Weeds Among the Wheat speaks to this reality.

> The kingdom of heaven may be likened to a man who sowed good seed in his field. While everyone was asleep his enemy came and sowed weeds all through the wheat, and then went off. When the crop grew and bore fruit, the weeds appeared as well. The slaves of the householder came to him and said, "Master, did you not sow good seed in your field? Where have the weeds come from?" He answered, "An enemy has done this." His slaves said to him, "Do you want us

to go and pull them up?" He replied, "No, if you pull
up the weeds you might uproot the wheat along with
them." (Mt 13:24–29)

There is a harsh realism to the Gospel sometimes.
The story is not one of a triumphant God entering human
history to rid the world of evil, banishing suffering and
turning all our tears to joy. It's a story of weeds and wheat
growing at the same time: suffering and joy, sorrow and
happiness—all requiring careful discernment and faith
that in the end, the lord of the harvest will bring forth fruit.

The Parable of the Weeds Among the Wheat is one
of Jesus' most realistic assessments of the human condition—and one that rings very true to any parent. Weeds
and wheat grow together in our lives: good and bad, hope
and sorrow, rejoicing and sorrowing. One day, our teens
may do well in a personal situation, and the next day, make
a poor choice that gets them into trouble. One day, Kris
shows selflessness in cleaning up around the house, and
the next day, he allows anger to get the better of him in
dealing with a sibling. But are we, as adults, really any
different? As we get older and recognize the consequences
of our actions, we ought to be better at avoiding sin and
growing in holiness. And yet the same flaws, rough edges,
and insecurities constantly rear their ugly heads, and we,
too, must throw ourselves upon God's mercy. Perhaps seeing our teens' flaws is difficult in part because they remind
us too much of our own. But perhaps in such times we
might become more aware of the abundance of that mercy.

The parable is about sin and judgment, and it points
to the way God will separate the weeds from the wheat at
the end of time. As such, it is one of several parables that

remind us that human life unfolds in a small window of history. All of our stories are part of a much longer story of what God is doing over time, and thus reminds us not to become too focused on ourselves. But it is also possible to read the parable as a commentary on the conflict we feel within ourselves—the pull between good and evil that faces all of us.

Keep Returning to Your Ignatian Toolbox

Our prayer, "Forgive us our trespasses as we forgive those who trespass against us," is a regular reminder of a theme found in several of Jesus' parables and teachings: namely, that God will judge us according to whatever yardstick we use with others. Jesus' frequent exhortations to the disciples to forgive again and again ("seventy-seven times") is a comment on how we must emulate the mercy of God. As parents, this is salutary advice. Teens will sometimes stretch our patience, and we need the reassurance that our regular need to forgive is part of our growth in holiness. Our teens are learning to discern the wheat in their lives from the weeds—and so are we. We can surely rejoice with them when they bring forth fruit; but when they get lost in weeds, we can just as honestly say "So do I, sometimes."

The human condition, according to the parable, is a place where both grow together. That's what we do—parents and teens—in this discerning age. One implication, then, is that we must help each other to become adept at seeing where the wheat is abundant. That is patient work. But it is also the work of holiness.

In our experience, being realistic about the growth of weeds and wheat means paying close attention to the bad and the good together—and especially looking for the good. In the face of difficulties, it takes some discipline to see the good. Recently, we were dealing with a serious issue with Kris—a really bad choice was made that has lasting implications. We had to take a long drive and really get to the bottom of the issue, and our minds were swimming as we tried to understand what exactly had happened. The issue has seriously impacted our relationship. It was a breach of trust and has made us much more wary of not being fooled easily. But in the midst of this difficult period, Kris scored a perfect grade on a chemistry test. We were delighted, since Kris had really struggled in that class. The opportunity to offer praise and congratulations amounted to a kind of island in the midst of a sea of otherwise difficult times.

Weeds and wheat grow together in our teens' lives. They may make terrible choices, but even still, they are capable of bringing forth fruit. Like God, we must recognize that sometimes an enemy sows wheat in our teens' lives. But also like God, we must be willing to seek the wheat and gather it conscientiously. We are stewards of our teens' lives, but not masters—only God is. As good stewards, our task is to be vigilant in the way we love, sometimes looking for wheat where there are many weeds. And we know that this kind of love can be transformative, even if it takes time.

Pause and Consider

1. What are examples of weeds and wheat that you see in your teen's life?

2. How about in your own life?

3. What are some ways you might pay more attention to the wheat in your teen's life, especially if, during this period, you see more weeds?

Do You and Your Teen Need Healing?

When life with our teens is hard, it is important to remember the place of healing in Jesus' ministry. From lepers, to the blind, to the woman with a hemorrhage, to paralytics, to those possessed by demons—Jesus reaches out in compassion to restore people to well-being. Early in Jesus' ministry, people flock to see him, captivated by his healing power and hoping that he will work miracles for them. What's interesting is that Jesus himself does not seem primarily interested in physical healing; he deflects attention from his healing power, several times telling people not to talk about it. One time, he even asks a blind man, Bartimaeus, what he wants Jesus to do. We imagine Bartimaeus saying to himself, "Duh!" (that is, "Isn't it obvious?" in teen speak)—but he answers, "I want to see." (Mk 10:51). And Jesus complies, saying it is his faith that has healed him.

Jesus is far more interested in calling people to a change of heart. He is willing to heal people's physical ailments as a way to draw them into faith and to show others what faith is like. A story that illustrates this dynamic is that of the blind man at the pool of Siloam.

> As he passed by he saw a man blind from birth. His disciples asked him, "Rabbi, who sinned, this man or his parents, that he was born blind?"
>
> Jesus answered, "Neither he nor his parents sinned; it is so that the works of God might be made visible through him. We have to do the works of the one who sent me while it is day. Night is coming when no one can work. While I am in the world, I am the light of the world." When he had said this, he spat on the ground and made clay with the saliva, and

smeared the clay on his eyes, and said to him, "Go wash in the Pool of Siloam" (which means Sent). So he went and washed, and came back able to see. (Jn 9:1–6)

Jesus indicates that the man's blindness is an opportunity to manifest God's works, to increase the faith of those who will be affected by the man's healing, including the man himself. After healing him, Jesus tells him to go to the local leaders and show them what has happened. But the incident causes a problem, because Jesus has healed him on a Sabbath day, when all forms of work (even healing) are prohibited by law. The incident causes division within the local leadership, and the formerly blind man is accused of being a sinner and eventually dismissed. Jesus seeks him out, consoles him, and reveals the real point of his ministry.

> When Jesus heard that they had thrown him out, he found him and said, "Do you believe in the Son of Man?"
>
> He answered and said, "Who is he, sir, that I may believe in him?"
>
> Jesus said to him, "You have seen him and the one speaking with you is he."
>
> He said, "I do believe, Lord," and he worshiped him.
>
> Then Jesus said, "I came into this world for judgment, so that those who do not see might see, and those who do see might become blind." (Jn 9:35–39)

Note that this very clear statement about who Jesus is comes only after the man has undergone healing and, after that, the equivalent of a congressional hearing. Jesus does not offer such a clear revelation of who he is to anyone in authority—not to the priests or members of the government—but rather to a once-blind man whom he describes as being someone who will manifest God's works. And he indicates here one of the many paradoxes throughout the gospels, that the blind are the ones who will see, while those with sight will become blind.

In this and many other biblical stories, the Lord reaches a person in spite of flaws, weaknesses, disabilities, or failures. God calls Moses, a man with a speech impediment (Ex 4:10), to lead his people out of Egypt. God calls Hannah, who is infertile, to bear a son who will become a great prophet. God calls Saul to be the king of Israel, a man whose lust for power ultimately is his undoing. God later calls David, the youngest of many brothers—any of whom appear to be a better candidate for being the king— and David later becomes an adulterer and a murderer. In Jesus' time, some of the most ardent of his followers are described as imperfect people: Matthew, the tax collector whom we met earlier; Peter, the uneducated fisherman who eventually denies he even knows Jesus; the woman who bathes Jesus' feet in her tears, described merely as "a sinner"; Mary Magdalene, the first witness to the Resurrection, who is described as someone "from whom seven demons had gone out"; and Paul, who before becoming an apostle mercilessly hunted and killed the followers of Jesus. God, it seems, does not reward perfection, but rather, seeks to heal our imperfections and thereby manifest his goodness.

Take Away

The best news for every parent is that God calls us as we are. We need not be perfect people to be great parents.

This is excellent news for parents of teens. We who are so aware of our teens' perfections and imperfections can be anxious about their futures, especially when life is hard. We who know more about the consequences of bad choices can hold onto great fears about who they are becoming. These stories about imperfection and healing are reminders that the way we see the world may indeed be blind and that those who see the world through their imperfections may, in fact, be closer to God.

There is another lesson in stories of healing, though—a very different lesson. It is that in these stories, Jesus sees people as God does. When the disciples asked what appeared to them to be an obvious question, whether it was the parents or the blind man himself who sinned, Jesus deflects their assumption. The man's blindness, he says, is not rooted in sin at all. What appears as an imperfection is nothing of the sort. To paraphrase Jesus' words to Peter in a different context, we are thinking not as God does but as human beings do. Jesus intimates that our perception of goodness can be skewed; what appears as sin may rather be a way that God reaches through a person's vulnerability. What his example suggests is that even hard times call for perspective: God sees our teens more fully than we can and is working through their vulnerabilities to soften their hearts. And because God always respects the freedom of his creatures, that process may take time. Our role is to never stop loving our teens, for that is a profound way that God does that slow work.

Pause and Consider

1. What sort of healing do you pray about for your teen?

2. What are the sources of pain or sadness that affect your teen's self-understanding?

3. As you meditate on the stories of Jesus healing others, what feelings, hopes, or desires for your teen emerge?

Righteous Anger and Moral Injustice

When we face difficult times as parents, it is easy to become angry—not necessarily at our teens but at what our teens face day in and day out. Our minds invariably fly to dark places of anger toward those who seduce our kids toward actions that we know are harmful. Our imaginations lash out at those who glamorize drug use or drinking; who show easy, consequence-free sex; who peddle products that capitalize on teens' natural body self-consciousness; who sell violent images; who normalize racism or misogyny. A great deal of our popular and even political culture treats the formation of children and teens as an afterthought, and so there are many ways that we can feel our anger flare up at the injustice we see visited on those we love.

It is helpful in these circumstances to remember the story of Jesus becoming angry and violent in response to injustice: the story of his cleansing the Temple of moneychangers. The story reminds us that anger itself is not sinful. The author of the letter to the Ephesians puts it well: "Be angry but do not sin; do not let the sun set on your anger, and do not leave room for the devil" (Eph 4:26–27). Anger is the right response to people who get in the way of God, making small things important and ignoring what ultimately will bring people closer to living as God has created them to live. Jesus gets to the heart of the problem: when people make money more important than God, evil follows.

> Jesus entered the temple area and drove out all those
> engaged in selling and buying there. He overturned
> the tables of the money changers and the seats of those
> who were selling doves. And he said to them, "It is
> written: 'My house shall be a house of prayer,' but you
> are making it a den of thieves." The blind and the lame
> approached him in the temple area, and he cured them.
> (Mt 21:12–14)

The Temple was an important gathering place for the
people of Israel, and those who were selling and buying
were people coming to offer the customary worship for
important life events such as the birth of a baby. Those
who sold doves were merely offering people the opportunity to buy what they needed for their offering in the
Temple, as prescribed by the law. Those who exchanged
money were offering a service to the people who came
from different parts of the region and used different forms
of money. Most people of Jesus' time, therefore, would
have perceived his action to be scandalous, even crazy.

There are two clues in this short text about what Jesus
was up to. The first is Jesus' own words, which emphasize
his desire to see that people treat the Temple not as a shopping mall but as a place of worshiping God. He quotes a
vivid line from the book of the prophet Jeremiah, calling to
mind God's desire that the Temple be a place of reverence.
Jeremiah's "Temple sermon," as it is called, went like this.

> Hear the word of the LORD, all you of Judah who enter
> these gates to worship the LORD! Thus says the LORD of
> hosts, the God of Israel: Reform your ways and your
> deeds so that I may dwell with you in this place. . . .
> Only if you thoroughly reform your ways and your
> deeds; if each of you deals justly with your neighbor;
> if you no longer oppress the alien, the orphan, and the

widow; if you no longer shed innocent blood in this place or follow after other gods to your own harm, only then will I let you continue to dwell in this place, in the land I gave your ancestors long ago and forever. But look at you! You put your trust in deceptive words to your own loss! Do you think you can steal and murder, commit adultery and perjury, sacrifice to Baal, follow other gods that you do not know, and then come and stand in my presence in this house, which bears my name, and say: "We are safe! We can commit all these abominations again!"? Has this house which bears my name become in your eyes a den of thieves? I have seen it for myself! (Jer 7:2–11)

Jeremiah's stern warning, and Jesus' recollection of it, point to a common theme in both the writings of the prophets and in the preaching of Jesus: God calls us to reform our hearts, to practice compassion toward "the alien, the orphan, and the widow"—rather than offer empty acts of worship. The other clue that Jesus offers in his cleansing of the Temple is in his welcoming of the blind and the lame. By law, they were prohibited from entering the Temple area, so Jesus' act of welcoming them—while effectively throwing out the buyers, sellers, and moneychangers—was a strong statement of who he believed could enter into the presence of the Holy One in the Temple.

The healings here are the last ones Matthew describes in his gospel, for it is not long after this event that Jesus is arrested and sentenced to death. This is the mature Jesus who has been emboldened by his profound sense of being on a mission; he is, to paraphrase John's version of the story, zealous for his Father's house, and he cannot tolerate those who pervert the intentions of the Lord for personal gain. Jesus is not acting out of control; his actions are measured. He performs what New Testament scholars call a *parabolic action*—that is, an action that functions similar to the way Jesus' parables do. Parables are colorful stories that deliver a point about God and God's kingdom; Jesus' action does the same thing. In this case, it says something like "the blind and the lame are closer to God than those who make money off others' piety!" Jesus wants to highlight the ways that people can fall into complacency—and even sin—and miss the edge of what God is calling his people to do in the world.

There is another way to consider the meaning of Jesus' cleansing the Temple, one which focuses on teens' developmental task of forming a moral conscience. In our work on college campuses, we've seen many examples of teens (fast becoming twentysomethings) calling attention to moral complacency that they witness among older adults. Students today are much more politically engaged compared to those of a generation ago, perhaps because of the ways that social media facilitate the formation of like-minded virtual communities. Sometimes this moral indignation is misdirected, and sometimes the way students demonstrate is ill-considered. But at the root of such demonstrations, we see young people trying to make sense of a world in which they perceive deeply rooted sin, much like Jesus. They are reaching for some kind of moral bedrock, some place where they can stand in right relationship to the world.

Often, we see, the thirst for justice is a proxy for religious practice. Many teens, in part because of the ways they are distancing themselves from their parents, will turn their critiques toward the Church itself, pointing to what they perceive to be its own injustices. The usual targets are sexual teachings or the role of women; less-nuanced critiques will be about historical issues like the Inquisition or the Crusades. One concern that we've raised, having sent our kids to both Catholic schools and public schools, is that some curricula are one-sidedly critical of the Church, painting a caricature of its history by focusing exclusively on its darker moments. Lost in these critiques are portraits of the saints and culture-builders who created the first universities and hospitals in the Western world; who introduced written languages in different missionary territories; who created financial structures to help the poor out of poverty; who provided leadership opportunities for women centuries before the modern women's movement; who made timeless contributions to the arts; who founded the science of genetics (Friar Gregor Mendel) and proposed the theory of the big bang (Father Georges Lemaître).

High school and early college-aged students are learning many things for the first time, and what they learn may awaken their consciences; this is very good. But in the words of Alexander Pope, "A little learning is a dangerous thing." Teens' first taste of justice is likely to reflect whatever bias is behind the presentation of an issue, and lacking any sense of the bigger picture, they are likely to embrace the good feelings associated with the prick of conscience. Often these awakenings will come through popular media—song lyrics, a particularly moving film, a documentary—which can be anywhere on the spectrum from profound truth to outright falsehood. Parents must be vigilant not only about what contributes to their teens' development of conscience but also about resources that might help them encourage their teens to learn more. Not everyone can be an expert on everything, of course—but it is still important to know the questions our teens are asking and to know where to point them for answers.

We believe that one of the Lord's great challenges to older adults is the moral indignation of emerging adults. Are they calling us to do more to address racism, economic disparity, urban violence, capital punishment, sustainability, or abortion? Good! We need to be challenged. In his 1,500-year-old guide to life in Christian monastic communities, Saint Benedict exhorted elders to listen to the young, "because it is often to the younger that the Lord reveals what is better." We are all prone to fall into patterns of thinking, habits of news-gathering, political tendencies, and so on. Young people see things with fresh eyes, and like Jesus, may focus more on the fundamental truth than on what is politically expedient. They will not always be right, but we will always be right by taking their conscience development seriously. We must learn to honor their emerging sense of justice while at the same time pointing them toward resources which will help them grow in knowledge and in faith.

For Reflection and Conversation

1. When do you experience anger at an injustice that has affected your teen? How have you expressed it?

2. What are examples of the ways your teen has felt anger toward an injustice?

3. What are some ways you seek to form your teen's conscience? How does your teen know that your conscience is already formed in this way?

4. What are some ways you can help your teen understand the Church's long history of moral reflection?

Consider the resources at the end of this book for some ideas.

Death and Resurrection

The absolutely unique part of the gospels, unlike any other ancient religious texts, is that they are a collection of stories that ultimately lead to a man's scandalous execution. We use the word "scandalous" here very deliberately: Saint Paul describes the Cross as a *skandalon* (Greek for "stumbling block"): "We proclaim Christ crucified, a stumbling block to Jews and foolishness to Gentiles" (1 Cor 1:23).

Paul is right: the Cross is a scandal. It's a stumbling block to anyone who wants to believe that life is really about being better than others or winning all sorts of acclaim and pats on the back. The problem we face as parents is that there are significant pressures for teens to assume exactly that. Many today live amid incredible stresses, not least of which include the pressures to perform academically or athletically. There are SAT scores to ace, résumés to build, jobs and internships to claim, and connections to be made. Amid these pressures, reminders of the Cross, the central symbol of Christian faith, seem crazy. Why follow someone who got killed?

The Cross, and what it represents, is important to us as parents for two reasons. First, it is God's way of saying to us, "Even in the midst of darkness, I am there. I will never abandon you, even in those moments when you feel terribly alone and your life's plan has backfired. I can bring life even where there is only death." Second, it is God's way of saying to your teens, "Do not count the successes of the world as the best measure of life. Sometimes the way of suffering is the way to freedom." In our lives, there have been moments when all we could do was simply to offer everything into God's hands, knowing that our efforts had led us to dead ends.

Christian spirituality, we suggested in our introduction—and Ignatian spirituality, in particular—is like falling into God's rhythm. It is about coming to a certain "feel" for the way that God acts in the world and seeks to draw people into relationship with him. There is a wrong way to interpret that rhythm, a way hinted at by Saint Teresa of Avila when, after God told her that he chastises his friends, quipped, "Then it's no wonder you have so few of them." Our tendency is to lay everything bad that happens upon God's shoulders. An alternate image, one closer to Jesus' own words in the gospel, is that when bad things fall upon our shoulders, God is there to share the burden. Difficult experiences can, paradoxically, become occasions for drawing closer to a God who seeks to heal us and lead us to freedom.

With teens, that promise can be at the same time a source of pain, for God never vetoes our freedom. And if the teen years are an age when a young person flexes his or her autonomy, that may in fact mean choosing to distance oneself from at least the perception of who God is or who the parents are. What we see is that young people will retain elements of the Gospel—such as a sense of justice, a conviction about not being a hypocrite, or a broad hope for world peace or fairness toward this or that group. All of these convictions, however unformed, are like seeds of a way of looking at the world that still bear meaning, and which, if allowed to germinate, would burst forth as a worldview that is at least consistent with the Gospel, if not fully embracing it. What's more, we've seen young people in the midst of renegotiating faith (or even rejecting what they know of it) who are willing to take on suffering for the sake of some greater good: serving in a volunteer program, entering selflessly into a relationship, or assuming a moral posture that requires some sacrifice of personal comfort.

The Cross is, among other things, a reminder to let God be God, and not to usurp that role. As Saint Ignatius suggests, it is important to "let the creator deal directly with the creature." We must never put a limit on God's forbearance and mercy; we must be willing to remember that every cross is a hint of the Resurrection. Life with teens will not always be easy, but with faith it will be a vocation of presence, of solidarity, and of willingness to embrace the cross. All those things are part of falling into God's rhythm.

A Closing Ignatian Meditation

Our final word is not about the difficulty in raising teens. It is about the joy of raising teens!

There is something magnificent about being part of daily and weekly dramas that constitute the unfolding of a sovereign creature's life in the face of eternity: before us is the unfolding of divine work, a beautiful human being the good Lord has given us the privilege to parent! Called to this vocation in life, we benefit from regularly reflecting on what it all means—to see our work as God sees it. This is the fruit of the regular practice of the examen. Rummaging through our day to see how God has been present, even in the midst of the ups and downs of daily life, reminds us that he helps carry our yoke, making our burdens light and sharing our joys.[1]

While daily reflection is an important dimension of Ignatian spirituality, there is a benefit to taking time to also do a more thorough inventory of our lives. Sometimes, life circumstances elicit such an inventory quite naturally: graduations, weddings, family reunions, and other big events help us to see the larger story of God's work in our lives. What we learn from Ignatius, though, is that it is possible and helpful to take time away, as Jesus did, to understand this larger story. Recall that Ignatius himself had this kind of experience when he went off to live in a cave and compose his Spiritual Exercises. Later, when he wrote his autobiography, he sought to pass on his life lessons. We, too, can benefit from the basic wisdom of taking a long, loving look at the arc of our lives, perhaps by spending a day or weekend away.[2] Even reflecting on our own experiences as teens may help shed light on the kinds of struggles and opportunities that impact our kids' lives today.

Becoming discerning parents ultimately means taking the time to allow our hearts to be softened and shaped by the God who, if given the opportunity, will create beauty in the world by virtue of our willingness to say yes. It means waltzing with God—remembering the image that Leah Libresco offered in chapter 1. It means devoting our lives to the kinds of prayer—regular interactions with the Lord—that befit busy parents. It means allowing our stories to be shaped by the story of Christ himself, such that our lives become a continuation of that story and an invitation to our teens to similarly be part of it. It means becoming adept at practicing ever-new ways of living out our faith in the context of family life, not ignoring difficulty but entering deeply into it, knowing that Christ wants to be present in it.

Therefore, as a final activity, we propose the following Ignatian exercise: an imaginative contemplation. This and others like it are ways of falling ever more deeply into God's rhythm. Give yourself the gift of learning those steps!

1. Find some time and space to relax and clear your mind. Choose a place where there will be no interruptions for thirty minutes. Stay with each of the following images, savoring them in your imagination and paying attention to what emotions they evoke.

2. Imagine the way God views the universe, and zero in on the small, blue planet where we now live. Consider it as God's garden amidst a vast cosmos.

3. Imagine God taking special pride in the creations he makes in this garden; view the whole of human history, from the emergence of human life through the advent of writing to the span of recorded history.

4. Now focus on the years allotted to you on this earth, and see your own life span through the eyes of the Creator. Imagine the plans God has made for your life, choosing you to be a parent who will one day share life with another person.

5. Now picture the way God sees your child, now a teen, and sees you parenting him or her. What does God see? What does God desire for you, whom he loves, and for your child, whom he loves?

6. Imagine the way God has created your child, your teen, to do some good in the world. Will he or she be a parent, too, one day? Will he or she take care of you in your old age? Consider the way God sees your teen interacting with others and laboring to draw him or her into intimate friendship.

7. Consider the way God sees your teen navigating the many challenges and obstacles he or she faces, knowing in the wisdom of mercy how difficult they can be. Rejoice with God at every success. Ache with God

at every failure. Imagine the way God moves the hearts of those who teach or coach your teen. Imagine the ways God seeks to incline the hearts of your teen and his or her friends, bending them toward just relationships and a just world. Consider how God draws your teen to imagine a future full of hope, laboring against those who would sow weeds to make him or her lose that hope. Imagine the way God has molded your own heart to help your teen navigate life's challenges, even when he or she reacts against your influence.

8. Now, see time in an instant: God seeing you and your teen as children, youths, and adults, even facing death. See the way God sees your teen throughout his or her life, moving from the teen years to adulthood and old age. Then, come back to where you are today, touching your teen's old age. You are parenting a future old man or woman, and you have the opportunity to shape the way this human creature touches others in the future. What are the lasting messages you want your teen to take with him or her toward adulthood? How do you want him or her to remember you when you die?

9. Pay attention to all the emotions that have emerged, and hold them before God in prayer. Conclude with gratitude that God has chosen you for the task of stewarding this young life toward adulthood. Pray that you may retain the graces of this exercise in the midst of the "now," whatever that may bring.

10. Conclude with an Our Father.

Resources

YouCat: Youth Catechism of the Catholic Church (San Francisco: Ignatius Press, 2010) is an adaptation of the *Catechism of the Catholic Church* specifically for teens and young adults. It's very readable and can be used in small chunks for conversation or even more formal instruction in parish-based classes (like Confirmation preparation or other religious education). Even the many one-liners sprinkled throughout the text make for great conversation starters or reminders around the house.

Busted Halo (bustedhalo.com) is the website of the Paulist Fathers dedicated to youth evangelization and formation. This site has been up for many years and has an impressive library of material ranging from questions about the Mass, to moral issues, to reflections on pop culture. While teens themselves may not seek out the site, parents might consider downloading or forwarding an article or two to pique a teen's curiosity or at least share a very accessible resource for thinking about things the way Catholics do.

Life Teen (lifeteen.com) is the Eucharist-centered movement in many parishes and dioceses around the country. Life Teen has developed a number of ministries to young people from middle school to college and offered programs and camps over many years. The website has links to good resources (books, videos) for teens, youth ministers, catechists, and others. It also has information about its missions that young people can join, conferences, camps, training opportunities for adults who work with teens, and social media outreach.

CovenantEyes: Internet Accountability and Filtering (covenanteyes.com) is a digital filter that allows parents to monitor and control online access for members of their households. Among other things, it allows parents to block access to pornography websites. It also has a blog about the consequences of porn.

Catholic HEART Work Camp (heartworkcamp.com) is a summer camp for teens who gather to undertake volunteer work and spiritual reflection. There are locations all over the country.

Real Life Catholic (reallifecatholic.com) is a ministry of Chris Stefanick focused on igniting a bold, contagious faith in the heart of Catholics, igniting them to share the beauty, power, and truth of the Gospel. Through live events, various media—including books, videos, and educational initiatives like Confirmation prep, Real Life Catholic draws teens into critical consideration of the Gospel.

Chastity Project (chastityproject.com) is the ministry of Jason and Crystalina Evert, introducing thousands of teens each year to a vision of sexuality rooted in the Gospel. Their blog, publications, social media presence, and speaking tour address contemporary questions teens are likely to ask (and many they are not).

Catholic Youth Bible (Winona, MN: St. Mary's Press, 2010) makes a great gift at Confirmation. It provides lots of footnotes and guides to reading scripture.

Blessed Are the Bored in Spirit (Cincinnati: Servant Books, 2006) by Mark Hart and *100 Things Every Catholic Teen Should Know* (Mesa, AZ: Life Teen, Inc., 2011) by Mark Hart and Todd Lemieux both feature a forthright style that holds great appeal for teen readers. Hart's many years in youth ministry, particularly as Executive Vice President for Life Teen International, have given him a feel for the challenges of reaching teens today.

Ablaze: Stories of Daring Teen Saints (Liguori, 2011) by Colleen Swaim shows that saints are the people who make clear what Christian faith does in ordinary lives. Swaim tells the stories of several relatively modern young men and women in ways that make teens imagine what it would be like to imitate their examples.

Take Ten: Daily Bible Reflections for Teens (St. Mary's Press, 2004) by Maureen Gallagher and Jean Marie Heisberger stands out among daily devotionals for teens. Many resources for daily Bible reflections assume older readers; this one does not. The short reflections are easily accessible, especially for those just learning how to dedicate some time to prayer. The title refers to the ten minutes expected for the daily reflections.

Prove It! series (*God, Jesus, Church, Prayer,* and *You,* all published by Our Sunday Visitor) by Amy Welborn aims at the average teen who may show indifference to Catholic faith and who may be challenged to think carefully through what the Church teaches. This series might be a first step for the unconvinced teen willing to be drawn into a good conversation. Welborn's books are organized as a series of books with short answers, good for teens not used to keeping sustained attention on an argument.

Notes

Introduction

1. Wilkie Au and Noreen Cannon Au, *The Discerning Heart: Exploring the Christian Path* (New York: Paulist Press, 2006).

1. How Can We Be Good Parents to Our Teens?

1. Sean Salai, S.J., "My Journey from Atheist to Catholic: 11 Questions for Leah Libresco," *America*, January 14, 2015, http://americamagazine.org/content/all-things/my-journey-atheist-catholic-11-questions-leah-libresco.

2. See, for example, Jessica Lahey, *The Gift of Failure: How the Best Parents Learn to Let Go So Their Children Can Succeed* (New York: HarperCollins, 2015) and Julie Lythcott-Haims, *How to Raise an Adult: Break Free of the Overparenting Trap and Prepare Your Kid for Success* (New York: St. Martin's Press, 2015).

2. Learning from Ignatius

1. Ignatius of Loyola, "The Autobiography," in George E. Ganss, S.J., ed., *Ignatius of Loyola: The Spiritual Exercises and Selected Works* (New York: Paulist Press, 1991), 70.

2. For modern adaptations of the *Spiritual Exercises*, see Tim's books *The Ignatian Workout* (Chicago: Loyola Press, 2004) and *The Ignatian Workout for Lent* (Chicago: Loyola Press, 2013).

3. Mark Thibodeaux, S.J., has a wonderful collection of different versions of the examen in *Reimagining*

the Ignatian Examen (Chicago: Loyola Press, 2015). For other resources for developing this practice of prayer see http://www.ignatianspirituality.com/ignatian-prayer/the-examen.

4. As suggested by the title of Philip Sheldrake's *Befriending Our Desires* (Notre Dame, IN: Ave Maria Press, 1994).

3. Helping Them Build Their Lives

1. Benoît Talleu makes these comments in "The Cradle of Life and Love: A Mother and Father for the World's Children," part of the Humanum video series, online at https://vimeo.com/ondemand/humanum.

2. See John Gottman, *The Marriage Clinic: A Scientifically Based Marital Therapy* (New York: W. W. Norton and Co., 1999), and J. Gottman and N. Silver, *The Seven Principles for Making Marriage Work* (New York: Three Rivers Press, 2000).

3. Maya van Wagenen, *Popular: Vintage Wisdom for a Modern Geek* (New York: Dutton Books, 2014).

4. The American Academy of Pediatrics website (www.aap.org) "recommends that parents establish 'screen-free' zones at home by making sure there are no televisions, computers or video games in children's bedrooms, and by turning off the TV during dinner. Children and teens should engage with entertainment media for no more than one or two hours per day, and that should be high-quality content. It is important for kids to spend time on outdoor play, reading, hobbies, and using their imaginations in free play."

5. See "Teens Suffer Highest Rates of FOMO," at http://www.psychology.org.au/news/media_releases/8Nov2015-fomo, reflecting on a November 2015 study.

6. See the April 2016 story at http://abc11.com/news/judge-sentences-war-vet-then-spends-the-night-in-jail/1303652.

7. See, for example, the Greater Good Science Center at the University of California at Berkeley: greatergood.berkeley.edu/article/item/the_poor_give_more.

8. See Tim's book *Come to the Banquet: Nourishing Our Spiritual Hunger* (Kansas City: Sheed and Ward, 2002), an invitation to teens and young adults to consider Christian spirituality through this metaphor of the banquet to which God invites us.

4. Freedom to Become Their Best Selves

1. Viktor Frankl's *Man's Search for Meaning* has been published in many editions over several decades and regarded by many as one of the most influential books of the twentieth century.

2. See, for example, the PBS *Frontline* special "The Merchants of Cool," which explores the tactics of manipulation used to push products to teens: http://www.pbs.org/wgbh/pages/frontline/shows/cool.

3. We share this story only to underscore the point that Kris observed something about God by observing us. We know too many single parents, many who are heroically raising children alone, to suggest that faith in God always means having a lasting marriage.

4. Two studies that point to parental influence on teens' choices about alcohol and drug use, for example, are at the National Institute on Drug Use at www.drugfree.org/join-together/commentary-teen-alcohol-use-parents-have-more-influence-than-they-think/ and the US Department of Health and Human Services' 2011 National Survey on Drug Use and Health at media.samhsa.gov/

data/NSDUH/2k10ResultsRev/NSDUHresultsRev2010.
htm.

5. See Tim's book *Seeds of Hope: Young Adults and the Catholic Church in the United States* (New York: Paulist Press, 2008) for a more extended reflection on the challenges of sharing faith with young people today.

6. The story of Bill Strickland is an example. See his remarkable book *Make the Impossible Possible* (New York: Crown Business, 2009), in which he describes his story of turning an interest in pottery into a school and eventually to a corporation that serves underprivileged young people in Pittsburgh. Manchester Bidwell Industries (http://manchesterbidwell.org) now has affiliates in a number of cities and has garnered Strickland a number of awards.

7. Arrupe said these words at a talk given to religious women in 1981, "Rooted and Grounded in Love," cited in Kevin Burke, S.J., "Love Will Decide Everything," *America*, November 12, 2007, http://americamagazine.org/issue/633/article/love-will-decide-everything.

5. The Gift of the Body

1. Michelle Yeomans, "Global beauty market to reach $265 billion in 2017 due to an increase in GDP," www.cosmeticsdesign.com/Market-Trends/Global-beauty-market-to-reach-265-billion-in-2017-due-to-an-increase-in-GDP.

2. We recommend the book *Wonder* by R.J. Palacio (New York: Knopf, 2012), a novel about a boy with a profound birth defect navigating middle school. We found it to be a good conversation starter about showing compassion at school.

3. See a good summary of Becker's work at the *Harvard Gazette*, March 19, 2009: http://

news.harvard.edu/gazette/story/2009/03/
fijian-girls-succumb-to-western-dysmorphia.

4. Hosea M. Rupprecht, F.S.P., *How to Watch Movies With Kids: A Values-Based Strategy* (Boston: Pauline Books and Media, 2011).

5. See Jacqueline Olds and Jerome Schwartz, *The Lonely American: Drifting Apart in the Twenty-First Century* (Boston: Beacon Press, 2009); John T. Cacioppo and William Patrick, *Loneliness: Human Nature and the Need for Social Connection* (New York: W. W. Norton and Co., 2009).

6. See Henry Kimball's summary, "American teens aren't nearly as lonely as their parents were, study says," at www.cnn.com/2014/11/24/health/teenage-loneli-ness-declines. The study he cites is that of D. Matthew T. Clark, Natalie J. Loxton, and Stephanie J. Tobin, "Declining Loneliness over Time: Evidence from American Colleges and High Schools," *Personality and Social Psychology Bulletin*, November 24, 2014, http://psp.sagepub.com/content/41/1/78.

7. See the 2015 US Bishops' letter on pornography, "Create in Me a Clean Heart," at http://www.usccb.org/issues-and-action/human-life-and-dignity/pornography/upload/Create-in-Me-a-Clean-Heart-Statement-on-Pornography.pdf. See also the anti-porn addiction website, www.fightthenewdrug.org.

8. See Tim Muldoon, "The Pedagogy of Friendship for Marriage," *Human Development* 30:4 (Winter 2010).

6. When Life Is Hard

1. Aristotle makes these observations in Book Eight of his *Nicomachean Ethics*.

2. See, for example, www.indiewire.com/article/sorry-ladies-study-on-women-in-film-and-television-confirms-the-worst-20150210.

Conclusion

1. See Dennis Hamm's fine treatment of the examen in "Rummaging for God: Praying Backward Through your Day," *America* May 14, 1994, reprinted at www.ignatianspirituality.com/ignatian-prayer/the-examen/rummaging-for-god-praying-backward-through-your-day.

2. As a practical note, many retreat centers around the country offer opportunities to practice spiritual exercises. Some, especially those run by the Jesuits (the Society of Jesus), root themselves explicitly in Ignatian spirituality.

Tim Muldoon is a theologian and the author and editor of several books on Ignatian spirituality, marriage, and family. He is the coauthor, with his wife, Sue, of *Six Sacred Rules for Families* and participated in the video production of *Joined by Grace*, the new marriage preparation program from Ave Maria Press. A professor for many years, Muldoon has taught at Mount Aloysius College and Boston College, and lectures and speaks frequently at colleges, universities, schools, parishes, dioceses, and retreat centers in the United States, Canada, and Europe.

Sue Muldoon is a therapist and religious educator who has worked in clinical, collegiate, and parish settings. Her clinical work has focused on young adults and children. She worked for many years in college counseling at Saint Vincent College and Saint Francis University, and she has worked as director of religious education for Good Shepherd Parish in Wayland, Massachusetts. Muldoon is the coauthor, with her husband, Tim, of *Six Sacred Rules for Families* and participated in the video production of *Joined by Grace*, the new marriage preparation program from Ave Maria Press. She and Tim have three children.

AVE

AVE MARIA PRESS

Founded in 1865, Ave Maria Press,
a ministry of the Congregation of
Holy Cross, is a Catholic publishing
company that serves the spiritual and
formative needs of the Church and its
schools, institutions, and ministers;
Christian individuals and families; and
others seeking spiritual nourishment.

———◦———

For a complete listing of titles from

Ave Maria Press

Sorin Books

Forest of Peace

Christian Classics

visit www.avemariapress.com

 AVE MARIA PRESS
Notre Dame, IN
A Ministry of the United States Province of Holy Cross